ELSEWHERE

One Woman,
One Rucksack,
One Lifetime of Travel

Rosita Boland

doubleday

TRANSWORLD PUBLISHERS
61–63 Uxbridge Road, London W5 5SA
www.penguin.co.uk

Transworld is part of the Penguin Random House group of companies
whose addresses can be found at global.penguinrandomhouse.com

Penguin
Random House
UK

First published in Great Britain in 2019 by Doubleday Ireland
an imprint of Transworld Publishers

A CIP catalogue record for this book
is available from the British Library.

ISBN 9781781620496

Typeset in 11.5/15pts Electra LT Std
by Integra Software Services Pvt. Ltd, Pondicherry

Printed and bound in Great Britain by Clays Ltd, Elcograf S.p.A.

Penguin Random House is committed to a sustainable
future for our business, our readers and our planet. This book
is made from Forest Stewardship Council® certified paper.

MIX
Paper from
responsible sources
FSC
www.fsc.org   FSC® C018179

3 5 7 9 10 8 6 4 2

For Lucy Corcoran
beloved niece and god-daughter

It is not down in any map; true places never are.

Herman Melville, *Moby-Dick*

Contents

FERNWEH

– an ache for
distant places

IN THE YEAR 2000, I bought the thirteenth edition of the Chambers Dictionary, and set myself a personal Millennium project of reading it cover to cover. Sometimes I wrote poetry, and poets are always searching for words that will go deep as wells.

There are 1,984 pages in the dictionary and I got through them all eventually, a few pages at a time, pen in hand. 'The richest range of English language from Shakespeare to the present day,' declared a sentence on its cover. As I read my way through the big red Chambers over the period of a year or so, I marked many obscure words I had never heard of; words that delighted me with the oddness and specificity of their precise definitions.

I had never known, for instance, that there is a word to describe a trail of damaged foliage created by a stag being hunted: *abature*. That a *dream hole* is a hole in the wall of a steeple for admitting light. That *leal* is true-hearted and faithful. That *parison* is a lump of glass before it's moulded into its final shape. That *metempsychosis* is the passing of a soul after death into some other body. That *mallemaroking* is the carousing of seamen in icebound ships. That to *guddle* is to fish with the hands by groping under the stones or banks of a stream. That *batology* is the study of brambles. That *knosp* is the unopened bud of a flower. That *vade-mecum* is a useful handbook that one carries about with one for constant reference.

I collected all these, and hundreds of others. I made my own dictionary, by writing the words and their definitions alphabetically into a Daler A5 hardback notebook. After each letter of the alphabet, I left some blank pages, so that I could continue to add to them over time. One weekend, when I had nothing much to do, I inexpertly cut out the letters of the alphabet from gold-flecked Japanese patterned paper and glued them down at the beginning of each section.

I thought of the notebook as my own *vade-mecum*, and hoped I would be able to periodically trawl through it for words to use in new poems in the future. In fact, I wrote only one more book of poetry, a couple of years after I made my dictionary, and then stopped entirely. The reporting I did in my daily job as a journalist was in some way both so immersive and endlessly satisfying in its variation that I somehow strayed far from thinking in poetry. Then I was gone too long; was too far away to pick up the vanished trail of breadcrumbs and return to the deep, verdant woods I had loved to linger in.

From time to time, however, I still take the notebook down and add a word to it; new words I come across. Like *fernweh*.

'Fernweh,' my multilingual friend Brian pronounced over dinner one night when we were out. We had been talking about travelling. 'That's what you have.'

'Fernweh?'

'It's a German word,' he said. 'The pain of not being in foreign parts. A desire to travel. An ache for distant places.'

Fernweh. *Fernweh*. So that's what it has been, all these years.

The proof of *fernweh* in my life stands on the top shelf of a bookcase in my kitchen-dining room: a row of black hardback notebooks. They are the diaries I have ritually kept since starting to travel aged twenty-two. I had saved up and travelled for long periods between jobs before I had a proper job. After that, I had managed lengthy periods of unpaid leave. My friend Róisín once asked me why I loved to travel so much. 'It's about being elsewhere,' I found myself saying. It has always been about being elsewhere. Whenever I came back to Ireland, the diaries I'd kept while elsewhere went up on a shelf with all the others, and there they had stayed. I had never reread these diaries, but I knew they were there if I needed to transport myself again to the places where they had been written, and that was enough.

I have diaries but no photographs, because I have never travelled with a camera. What I do have are folders of paper ephemera: boarding passes, maps, banknotes, museum admission tickets, trekking passes, guesthouse receipts, postcards and many other items that individually seem inconsequential, but collectively form the palimpsest of a lifetime's wandering.

What I also have are my passports with their arcane interior mosaics of many stamps and visas. I love those various passports almost to the point of fetishism; my evidence of portals to elsewhere. I even searched for years for a special box to keep them in, eventually finding it by chance a few years ago in an art gallery in Ennistymon, Co. Clare.

It is a small rectangular wooden box made by the artist's husband from salvaged wood, which she had then painted deep shades of cobalt and midnight blue, interspersed with silver stars. The main image is of a wingéd red-haired woman, wearing only boots, on a silver horse, flying through the blue starry night. I have red hair. It is corny as hell, but I didn't care. This box was meant to be mine. I bought it without knowing if the passports would fit or not. They did: dropping cleanly into the empty box and filling it perfectly, like the missing piece of a puzzle. The box now stands on a shelf in my living room, and every time I look at it, it makes me feel happy.

In the days after that dinner, I found myself constantly repeating the perfect new word Brian had given me. *Fernweh*. I could not get it out of my head.

One weekend, not long after our dinner, I was visiting my parents. It was a Sunday, and Sundays mean my father's delighted tussle with the fiendish *Sunday Business Post* crossword that he rarely fails to complete, despite now being into his nineties. That day, he had a dictionary beside him on the table, the one that had belonged to his mother.

I recognized this book. I had often taken it from my father's study as a child to look up some word for homework. My grandmother had died long before I was born, but I knew this had been her book, and as it was one of the very few things in the house that I knew had belonged to her I had always regarded it with particular fondness. That Sunday, as I lifted the dictionary from the table to look up a word for my father, I realized with a surge of pleasure that it too was a Chambers.

Katherine Boland's dictionary was the third edition of the Chambers, and had been published in 1909. It was a faded red hardback, now missing its spine, with a stylized art nouveau cover. The flyleaf read: 'Pronouncing, explanatory, etymological, with compound phrases, technical terms in use in the arts and sciences, colloquialisms, full appendices and copiously illustrated.' The copious illustrations were tiny, exquisitely detailed line drawings scattered through the pages: a spiritsail ship, a quincunx arrangement, a marquis's coronet, a gargoyle, a jester's bauble.

That afternoon, as I carefully turned its pages for the first time in decades, I realized with a jolt that someone had marked the word *abature* with a fine nib in faded black ink. That had been the very first word I had marked in my own Chambers, when starting to read my way through it, all those years before. I stared at the page, transfixed.

Before I left that weekend, I asked my father if I could borrow the book, and took it back with me. At home in Dublin, I took first my own Chambers down from a bookshelf, and then the notebook with the dictionary of words I had made from it. I opened up my notebook. There it was on the first page, *abature*. I read the definition again. Something struck me. I went back to my grandmother's dictionary.

The definition of *abature* in the 1909 dictionary, a word I like to believe my grandmother had herself marked for some long-lost reason, was, 'The trail of a beast of the chase.' In my 1999 Chambers it is, 'In hunting, the trail through underwood beaten down by a stag.' I put the dictionaries down, stirred and thrilled. It was the linguistic equivalent of seeing fast motion photography. The distance of ninety years was encompassed in those two definitions.

I knew of course that new words are regularly being introduced to the English language all the time, to reflect elements of our ever-changing lives. But it had never occurred to me that words established in the lexicon for almost a century could have definitions that shift with the passing of time. My dictionary was very specific about the particular kind of beast which left a trail when being chased: a stag. At some point in the intervening years, someone at Chambers had decided that they were going to focus the definition of *abature* still further. But how did they decide this? Why did the definition change? When did the stag become part of it?

I hunted on through the pages, making my own trail of pencil marks in the dictionaries, cross-referencing a number of definitions of the words I had selected back in the year 2000. Some were the same, but some, like *abature*, were distinctly different, as if an aperture had opened out and the definition had mysteriously developed over time. I closed the books and sat there for a while in my kitchen. It felt like some cipher had been decoded that I hadn't even realized I was searching for.

My gaze travelled upwards to the shelf where the record of my *fernweh* life stood. I had never reread any of those diaries, but I had always meant to do so some day. Sitting there, I found myself wondering what it would be like to return to the past, now that I was so far from the person I had been when I made those journeys.

Would I find, as in the two Chambers, separated by their distance of ninety years, that the intervening time had created some kind of sorcery; that in the years between what I had recorded at the time and now a new truth had quietly evolved and developed; that there was, after all, something significant to be discovered by looking back?

I took down the diaries and, finally, I began to read them.

Australia
1988

ELEUTHEROMANIA

\- an intense desire
for freedom

IN THE EVENINGS at Crocodylus, there was always Lou. Lou lived nearby, and was often in Crocodylus. He was small and wiry, with a moustache, and was never without his battered Akubra hat. Although small in stature, he often gave the impression of occupying a much larger space than he did, fading in and out of company like a chameleon. His politeness when he had initially met me off the plane didn't last. He tossed swear words into conversation like grenades.

'Don't fucking call me your mate, Rosita. I'm not your fucking mate, right? I don't know you.'

'Fucking rain again.'

'No fucking business today again.'

I had stumbled upon Crocodylus by chance. It was 1988, and I was nearing the end of a year travelling in Australia. I had flown into Daintree from Cookstown, on a tiny Cessna plane, into a field the jovial pilot told me had to be cut back regularly, otherwise the rainforest would reclaim it.

'Where are you off to now?' he enquired, lifting out my rucksack for me from a hatch at the side of the plane.

'I'm not sure,' I said, looking around uncertainly. The plane had literally landed in the middle of a cleared field surrounded by tall, lush vegetation, and I could see no sign of anything. It wasn't an airport, as such; more a bush landing.

'There's someone over there,' the pilot said, waving to a man who had just drawn up in a jeep. The someone turned out to be Lou, who had come from Crocodylus to meet the plane, and tout for business.

'You want a ride to Crocodylus?' he asked.

'What's Crocodylus?'

'It's a new place. Come have a look anyway. There are other places nearby if you're not keen.'

Crocodylus was a brand-new little eco resort, built in the middle of the Daintree rainforest. It had opened only weeks previously. The resort consisted of a number of simple huts around a small saltwater pool. They were wooden structures built on stilts, to lift them off the rainforest floor, and were connected by raised wooden walkways. The huts had kelly-green canvas walls, with rectangular holes cut out of them and covered with mosquito netting for windows. Each was named for an Australian native tree. My hut, the women's dorm, was Candlenut. My top bunk was the one closest to the mosquito-netting window. Lying there at night was like camping, the world beyond only a thin membrane away.

The rainforest cover was a living parasol. When I went outside, it felt like stepping into a different world, a brighter one, where the light was hard and it took time for my eyes to adjust. Crocodylus seemed to be the essence of green; everything in and around it was lush and exotic and growing as I watched. Most afternoons that September, it rained at two o'clock for an hour, the rain falling down like fluent, watery lianas through the canopy of green. The air felt disturbed and primitive after it had rained; somehow feral.

I had been beguiled by Crocodylus on arrival. It had not taken me long to spot a sign saying 'Workers wanted in exchange for free food and board.' Right away, I had signed up, although it was now less than a fortnight to my flight back to Ireland, which was departing from Sydney, a couple of days' travel south. I pushed my imminent departure to the back of my mind, and tried to live in the moment.

The work was not difficult. I served breakfast in the morning, and dinner in the evening, cleaning up the kitchen afterwards. After breakfast, I cleaned the private huts, changed the linen, and did the laundry. One morning, barefoot, I swept out a large scorpion from under the bed I had just stripped. Its tail was flicked back, ready to strike. I had brought it to within an inch of my right foot. I swept it through a crack in the floorboards, where it fell into the gullet of green under the huts to join all the other creatures and reptiles and insects I knew were moving there but hardly ever saw.

A generator powered the complex, and usually went off about midnight. All the electricity ran off the generator, and every night, when it was turned off, the rainforest became the darkest and loudest of places, with nocturnal animals scuffling in the unseen undergrowth. We had torches, for night-time visits to the toilet blocks; a trip I rarely made without seeing eyes staring at me, their reflection caught in the light of my torch.

Every morning before starting work at 7 a.m., I went for a run or walk on the beach. During those early mornings, I thought constantly about returning to Ireland. Before arriving in Australia, I had graduated with a degree in Modern English and History, after four years of university life I had not much enjoyed. I had just turned twenty-three, and still had no idea what I was going to do for a living on my return. I had a vague notion about making writing a career, although in what way, I couldn't see. I wrote poetry, but knew that was a genre that was never going to support me, and I wasn't sure if I could ever write anything else; fiction, for instance. Besides, I knew many Irish writers, and almost none of them earned enough to support themselves by writing alone, no matter what genre they worked in.

I was sure about one thing, though: I did not want to live in Dublin, or Ireland, for the foreseeable future; perhaps never again. I felt that in many ways my life had only truly started when I had got off the plane in Sydney, all those months ago. The sensation of freedom and distance from everything and everyone I knew had been thrilling in its totality. I loved everything about being a person from somewhere else, and the way that all around me was new and different, from the consistently hot weather to the fact that the Plough had been replaced in the night sky by the Southern Cross; a constellation that to this day rejuvenates me whenever I see it, because it tells me I am far, far from Ireland. In Australia, I felt I could truly breathe for the first time in my life; could start exploring the person I might become, whoever that was going to be.

As I ran and walked on the beach before starting work for the day, I knew again what I had already known for months: what I really wanted to do next was to find a way of extending my visa, so I could stay another year in Australia. My job in Crocodylus was open-ended: I had been told it was mine for as long as I wanted, and I wanted very badly to keep it as long as possible. Yet at some time in those mornings, I finally admitted to myself it was in fact far too late for me to extend my visa: one of my siblings was getting married in Ireland the following month, and I had promised before even going to Australia that I would return in time for the wedding. To not go back would cause all sorts of consternation.

The greater part of my days at Crocodylus was free. There were two other backpackers around my age working there too: a Scottish man called Kevin and an Australian woman called Jo. We worked different hours, but were all generally free in the afternoons. Every day we went together to a pool at the bottom of a nearby waterfall, or to a secluded small beach almost an hour away, which was not accessible by road. It had the improbable, but real, name of Robinson Crusoe beach, and we got there by crossing another beach and then trekking through a path in the rainforest.

We were always the only people on Robinson Crusoe beach. It was ridiculously, wildly, picturesque. The deserted beach was curved; framed on one side by the dense greenery of the rainforest, and on the horizon by an endless-seeming empty blue ocean. We never once saw any boats out there. The happiness I felt when emerging from the dim cool rainforest on to the bright sand, the cerulean sea aglitter in the sunlight, was a pang of pure joy I still recall, all these years later. I've never looked it up on Google Images, but you can. I want to leave it as unretrieved buried treasure in my memory. Even now, whenever people talk about paradise beaches, I see Robinson Crusoe's deserted beach in my head; the lush rainforest right behind, the empty blue sea in front, expanding into the horizon like our whole lives that lay ahead of us then.

And in the evenings, there was always Lou. Lou knew the owners of Crocodylus, and soon enough, he knew us too, adapting easily to us newcomers. I would be back in Ireland within a fortnight; Jo would stay a little longer, and then she would be gone, too – back to Melbourne. Kevin was leaving soon after me, heading home to Glasgow. We were on borrowed time, thrown together in the kind of on-the-road friendships that only last days, and yet the four of us hung out together as if we were comfortable old friends. Every evening, after Kevin, Jo and I finished our jobs, we gathered at a small table in a corner of the clearing and steadily drank our way through the many carafes of free red wine that came with our board. Lou scorned the wine, drinking only beer.

One evening Lou brought his three dogs into Crocodylus. They were the biggest dogs I had ever seen in my life. They looked like Great Danes, crossed with wolves. Pale brown in colour, they looked almost leonine, as if they truly belonged on the savannah of Africa rather than the lush rainforest of northern Australia.

Lou brought them up to us one by one. Enormous tongues licked my hand. Then the dogs flopped together in a huddle of bones and muscle and tails on the rainforest floor, like the collective makings of a dinosaur skeleton. One yawned, and I saw a flash of sharp white teeth before its jaws snapped shut.

'What are their names, Lou?' I asked.

'Brick, Meathead and Nunya,' he incanted, and each dog looked up briefly as its name was mentioned.

'Why is Nunya called Nunya? Is it an Aboriginal word? What does it mean?'

Lou grinned. 'I'm so glad you asked me that,' he chuckled. 'Because it's none-ya-fucking-business.'

Brick, Meathead and Nunya were not pets. They were Lou's working dogs, and he took them with him on boar hunts into the rainforest, where thousands of boars had gone feral. He showed me the collars that they wore when working. Specially made hinged wooden collars, they were tall and wide as a man's handspan.

'See this?' Lou said, putting one into my hand, where it weighed heavily. 'The dogs wear these fucking things when we go hunting, right?'

'Right.'

'They have to have these on, because when they go in for the kill, the fucking boar will try to go for their jugular, right?'

'Right.' The collar I was holding was Meathead's. It was heavy, carved from solid wood, its outer surface scuffed and splintered; all that had lain between the skin of the hunter and the teeth of the hunted.

He wanted to turn his ad hoc boar hunts into a business. He'd taken out friends, who told him he should experiment with the idea. 'I'm going to get these fucking tourists out into the rainforest with my dogs, and they won't know what's fucking hit them.'

Lou was not doing any trade in his boar hunts. Night after night, he sat with us, moaning – or, more accurately, cursing – about business. As Crocodylus was newly opened, and, in that pre-internet era, word had still not spread about this little eco resort in the rainforest, the place was quiet. Apart from a few backpackers like us, the only guests were occasional couples. The women had nice hair and many sets of bikinis and were not living out of rucksacks. The men looked clean cut and wore shades, even in the dim rainforest.

The couples wandered around hand in hand, or lay on the beach in the afternoons, but they never made it to our beach at Robinson Crusoe. They either didn't know about it, or couldn't be bothered to walk that far. They stayed in the pricier, private huts, usually for two nights at most. They more or less recoiled when they saw Lou in the evenings, with his weathered skin, battered hat, and huge intimidating dogs, as he went around the dinner tables, touting for boar hunt business.

One evening Lou came to our table grinning widely. He slapped his Akubra down on the table. He had news for us. 'Guess what?'

'What, Lou?' I asked.

'Screw them,' he said, waving his hand dismissively in the direction of that evening's assortment of couples, sitting at tables nearby; quite near enough, in fact, to be within earshot. 'We're getting some real sons of bitches here soon.'

Lou told us that the owners had just received their first block booking for all the huts in the resort. A New South Wales rugby team who were having an unexpectedly good season were coming for two days' down time from training. They would be arriving the day after tomorrow, when Crocodylus had been cleared of all its other guests, apart, of course, from Kevin, Jo and me. It would be Lou's big opportunity to do some business; soliciting money from an entire rugby team, plus whatever supporting entourage they had. He was gleeful; for Lou, he was almost cheerful.

'I'm going to get every last one of those fuckers out into the forest with me,' he declared.

He told us he would not be hanging out with us the first night the team would be in Crocodylus, because he would need to sit with them over drinks and 'schmooze' them, as he put it. I had only known Lou a few days, but I was pretty sure he was incapable of schmoozing. Goad, provoke, challenge, yes. Schmooze, no.

Over the next day and a half, everyone who had been staying in Crocodylus departed. The three of us were busy, getting laundry done and all the huts ready. There was a lot of extra sweeping and cleaning and maintenance of the partially open-air bar and dining area; for once, there was nobody there for

us to work around. As the incoming party was so large, three
tables were put together to form one long outdoor surface. We
made sure our usual little round table was left in a corner of
the clearing, where we could see everything that was going
on. We had been promised extra free drinks for the extra work
we'd done.

That evening, some time before dusk, a string of vehicles
drew up and offloaded the team and their minders. They
exploded into the clearing in a burst of noise and activity.
There were about twenty of them, but at first it seemed as
if there were many more. It was soon evident that the 'eco
resort' of Crocodylus was not the kind of resort they had been
expecting.

'Where's the casinos?'

'Where's the sheilas?'

'Where's the fucking action, mate?'

As soon as they had found their huts and dumped their
stuff, they headed for the bar. The bar at Crocodylus was tiny,
no more than the length of two breakfast counters, half in, half
out of shelter. The group stood around it with their beers, while
I took the food orders. Jo and I were the only women on-site
that night, and as a result, we attracted much attention.

'Doing anything tonight?'

'Love the Irish accent. Can I hear more of it later?'

'You're the two best-looking women in Queensland right
now!'

We slapped them off with the unselfconscious ease we
used when slapping off the mosquitoes that hummed persistently in a permanent layer between the rainforest floor and the
canopy of the damp lush greenery far above. We knew they
were only kidding. They had been fooled into thinking they

were coming to a big fancy Queensland casino resort, with entertainment laid on, and instead they had got empty, tiny Crocodylus, in the middle of the rainforest. Once they had got over the joke, they started to enjoy themselves. They might have landed in a place where there was only one woman to ten of them, but they had also got Lou, with his big plans for them the following day, and who winked at us as he arrived.

Dinner was raucous that evening. Lou sat with the team, matching them beer for beer. I don't know what it was he said, but at one point heads around the table collectively snapped in his direction. He was gesticulating with his hands, talking fast, and then everyone else was, too. There was laughter, and much thumping of the table. Someone shook his hand. Someone else high-fived him. He turned to look for us and gave a thumbs-up. Lou's boar hunt was finally happening.

The following morning, when Lou arrived in his large pick-up truck, Brick, Meathead and Nunya were already wearing their wooden collars. The dogs were exceptionally loud and active that morning, as if they knew from the weight around their necks what lay ahead. The players jumped up on the back of the pick-up, taunting the worst of the hung-over stragglers, who were the last to emerge from their huts. The generator had stayed on long past midnight, and the bar had had its best night's business since opening.

'Feeling crook, mate?' This was said with relish, not sympathy.

'You can chunder over the side if you need, mate, just get your fat hairy arse over here.'

'Garn get fucked, ya mongrel,' one of the stragglers retorted, looking green in the face.

When they were gone, the rainforest seemed eerily still, its silence tight as the surface of a drum. The place was empty. For the first time ever, we did not go to the waterfall or to Robinson Crusoe beach that afternoon when we had finished our jobs. We did not want to miss the return. I had torn one of my few shirts, and I sat on the verandah of Candlenut that afternoon, primly sewing, feeling like a character in a Victorian novel. Jo read a book in her bunk. Kevin, who had come to join me on the verandah to chat, eventually lay down and fell asleep.

It rained again that afternoon, and the sound of the rain coming through the leaves was louder than ever, without the usual background noise of people coming and going from their huts. I put the mended shirt down and sat there on the verandah, listening to the rain. The thought of leaving this place that I had come to love so much in so short a time made me feel something like panic. I was not ready to go home, and I did not want to leave, but I knew I could not put off the final leg of my year-long journey. In two days, three at the most, I would have to start heading south for Sydney.

In the very late afternoon, just before dusk, we heard the sound of people shouting in the distance. We all gathered together in the clearing, listening. As the sound came closer, we could hear it more distinctly: it was like a bellow that came and went in volume like an animal howling.

Lou's pick-up truck drove into the clearing, the horn blaring. The dogs jumped off the back first, no longer wearing their collars, and Lou hopped out of the cab. He still looked fresh and full of energy, and pretty much as he had when he set off that morning. The rugby players tumbled off the back of the pick-up one by one. Most of them now had filthy clothes. Their legs and arms were scratched and muddy. Their hair was wild. They all looked exhausted but they also had something else in common: they looked ecstatic.

Just one man remained standing on the back of the truck, holding an object high up in the air. He was shouting something and the others were cheering, but I wasn't listening. I was looking at what was in his hands. It was the severed head of a boar. Eyes half open, it was far bigger than the size of his own head, with its huge tusks and teeth visible. This man held it aloft like a trophy, as if he was the captain of their team. Perhaps he was.

That evening, I took dinner orders, as I had done every night since arriving.

'I'll have the steak. Make that two steaks. I'm famished!'

'Two steaks here too.'

'Yeah, me too. Boar hunting is hungry work.'

'Does everyone who's having steak want two steaks?' I asked, when I was halfway round the table. They did. They were drinking with wild, celebratory abandon. When I had put the orders into the kitchen, I fetched more beers, bottles of wine, and two bottles of tequila from the bar. There was not a lot of spare room on the table, because in the centre of it was the boar's head, balancing on a collar of its own dried blood. Every time I looked at the severed head, I felt as if I was hallucinating.

When I was finished serving, I went to sit with the others. They were already a couple of carafes down, both of them staring at the boar's head.

'Can you fucking believe that thing?' Kevin said.

'Wine, please,' I said.

We got slowly thrashed sitting there, all of us staring, mesmerized, at the head. We were waiting for Lou to finish dinner and tell us what had happened. Eventually, he got up and came over to us, the dogs padding after him, flopping down with loud sighs.

'So we got us a fucking boar,' he said, enunciating each word with slow satisfaction. He was even drunker than we were. He told us he had taken the players deep into the forest and made them run in different pointless directions for his entertainment, until they were knackered. By then, the dogs had got the scent of a boar. He made everyone run again after the dogs, as they tore off barking and howling.

'We found the fucker. Cornered it. Set the dogs on it.' It was Brick – now snoring and twitching beside us – who had gone in for the kill. Lou had started the job of severing the head with his knife, and the others had taken turns to finish it. They'd left the body behind in the forest, for other animals to eat. 'Cheers,' Lou said, lifting his wobbling beer glass, and clinking ours. He was feeling uncharacteristically sentimental. 'You're not bad fuckers as tourists go, ya mongrels,' he said, toasting us, as we refilled our own glasses.

As the night progressed, everyone got colossally drunk. The more drunk the players got, the more daring they were with the boar's head. It was taken from its place on the table, and passed around from hand to hand, first cautiously, then with ever more bravado. There was talk of an impromptu rugby match, using the head as a ball. People were yelling. We were yelling. I was yelling. We were all out of our minds.

Then someone made a move to claim the head. Something glinted. I watched transfixed as the stiffened jaw was levered open with a knife. People were on their feet, cheering. The blade appeared and disappeared, as tooth after tooth was hacked out from the boar's jaws.

'Souvenirs!' someone called, as the chips of bone flew around the rainforest like enamel fireworks. They vanished into the darkness beyond the fringes of the light that the generator cast.

Suddenly I was on my feet, drunkenly staggering forward, propelled by an urgency that was overwhelming me. I wanted one of those teeth. In a week, I would be back in Ireland, and I wanted one of those teeth as a reminder of what life could be like elsewhere. I was already afraid I might forget this year and the freedom it represented; afraid that I might never go anywhere again. I was, above all, afraid nothing would ever happen to me again.

Then the managers decided to put a stop to the night. It was long, long after midnight. One of them came over to warn us they were turning off the generator in five minutes, as they wanted to get everyone to bed. Lou decided to crash in his pick-up with the dogs for the remainder of the night. The three of us stumbled to the toilets and then fell into our bunks. Everything had been chaotic, and I was so wired that I had not in fact managed to retrieve a tooth.

Suddenly the lights went out. A roar went up. The lights stayed out. Gradually, the players realized they were not coming on again and started making a move towards their huts. Jo and I heard people laughing and running past our hut and into the night, deep into the rainforest where we were not meant to go alone in darkness.

'We're going on another boar hunt!' one man yelled, and others cheered.

The noise was incredible. I heard people crashing through the vegetation, and nocturnal creatures and birds squawking. In the darkness, they were falling off the raised walkways, on to the rainforest floor. Lying there drunk in my bunk, I imagined the rainforest opening its jaws and swallowing everyone up in its great green maw. Briefly the lights went on again, and the managers went grimly to fetch their errant guests back, using language even Lou would have admired.

In the morning, I woke at eight, two hours later than usual, my head pounding. The players were gone. Lou was gone. The head was gone. I searched the clearing floor and the nearby rainforest boardwalks. I wanted one of those boar's teeth like I had never wanted anything in my life. I searched and searched, but found nothing.

England
1990

WUNDERKAMMER

- a cabinet
of curiosities

AT THREE DIFFERENT times in my life, I lived in London. London, for me, was always about earning enough money to go elsewhere. I was always coming back from somewhere, flat broke, and planning the next escape.

The second time, I was twenty-four, and was not long returned from Australia. I had my first proper job, working for a publishing company as an editorial assistant. It was a permanent position but, although I didn't say so in the interview, I never had any intention of staying long. Soon after joining, I was invited to a meeting with the organization who managed the company pension fund. The man from Scottish Widows – a name I found thoroughly bizarre – instructed me solemnly in what I should expect to make by way of pension in the future after my theoretical decades of service. I stifled an inappropriate desire to laugh aloud. I had no idea what the future held for me, but I knew I would not be cashing in a Scottish Widows pension some forty years hence. Even the thought of it made me feel anxious and trapped.

I didn't want a long-term job at that time in my life, no matter what it was, and the publishing job was a good one, with excellent 'prospects'. I didn't care. Part of me, the grave and thoughtful part, worried that I was being reckless about failing to build a career, but most of me, the impulsive and instinctual part, simply didn't care. I only wanted the freedom to be able to earn some money and then leave to go travelling again. I wanted to try and repeat, as often as possible, the experience I had had in Australia. I fully expected to be living a life where I did not have a career as such; more a succession of different short-term jobs, and that was just fine by me.

For the first part of that year, I lived in the upper half of a house in Agar Place, Camden Town. Heavy goods trains that only ran at night pounded through to nearby King's Cross, and sometimes shook me awake, but I liked feeling part of a city where things were happening all the time.

Between the books we published, some of which I took home, and the many books I bought myself, my attic room was like a paper eyrie. They were all in stacks on the floor, because there were no bookshelves. I like order, and the towers of stacked books that regularly collapsed like literary masonry on to the bedroom floor drove me mad.

The flat had an absentee landlady, and her sister was my flatmate. After some negotiation, it was agreed that a modest sum would be provided for me to buy a set of second-hand bookshelves, as long as I could arrange for their delivery. Neither myself nor my flatmate had a car or could even drive.

I went about perusing the pale orange pages of *Loot*. At that time, it was the go-to small-ads publication in London for anyone looking for anything, whether a job, a flatmate, a car, a puppy, or a set of second-hand bookshelves.

I found many ads for bookshelves, but none that also offered delivery. I persisted, and eventually found an ad for bookshelves on sale for £25. They were located in Primrose Hill, which was not far from Camden, but more importantly, free delivery was included. I called the number. A man's voice answered. I vaguely registered that he seemed old, or as old as anyone seems when you are twenty-four, and cannot imagine being even thirty.

It was agreed that I should call to the apartment on Saturday at 11 a.m., and that if the bookshelves proved suitable, he would drive me back to Camden with them.

At the appointed time that Saturday, I stood outside a red-brick mansion block of apartments, and rang the bell. The door buzzed, and I took the old-fashioned cage lift up to the third floor and knocked on the door to the left of the lift, as instructed.

When the door opened, two things struck me immediately. One was that the door opened so swiftly that the man who opened it must have been standing directly behind it, waiting for my knock. He was standing alongside a woman whom he introduced as his wife. The second thing that struck me was that they seemed markedly over-dressed for eleven on a Saturday morning. The man wore a white shirt, a cravat, and a waistcoat. The woman wore a taffeta skirt in dark blue. They were both silver-haired, and perhaps in their seventies, I thought, although I have never been good at guessing people's ages. All I knew was that they seemed very much older than me.

Their names were Henry and Margaret. Margaret took my coat, and then they proceeded to give me a tour of their apartment. I was shown the galley kitchen, the small bathroom, and the one bedroom. I stood in the doorway and stared at their double bed, with its red candlewick bedspread folded back from the white pillowcases. There was a reproduction of Constable's *Hay Wain* on the wall over the bed, and a pair of bedside lockers, one on either side. The bed was neatly made, but from under one of the pillows a stray pyjama leg extended.

I could not stop looking at it. The pyjama leg was an almost unbearably intimate detail of their lives.

I had no idea why I was being shown their entire home. I had never bought anything through the small ads before, and if there was an unwritten code of conduct that went along with it, I did not know what it was.

Eventually I was shown into the sunny living room, where an empty three-shelved bookcase awaited my inspection. It was perfectly fine. I was invited to sit down. Evidently, the free delivery wasn't going to happen any time soon. I sat, regretting this odd expedition more with every passing second.

'Sherry?' Henry asked. It was more of a statement than a question.

'Of course she'll have a sherry,' Margaret said. 'I'll have one too.'

I took the glass of sherry offered to me, because I did not know what else to do. I perched on the edge of their sofa and they relaxed back into two armchairs, holding their glasses out like people at a cocktail party, while grilling me politely but extensively about my life.

'How long have you been in London?'

'Where are you working?'

'Do you like your job?'

'What do you make of the city?'

'You're Irish, aren't you?'

'Where are you from in Ireland?'

'Do you miss your family back home?'

I answered their questions with a growing sense of bewilderment. I had a line of sight out to the hallway, and it struck me, as I sat there awkwardly sipping sherry I did not want, that I had heard the door being locked and bolted after my entrance. It also struck me that nobody knew where I was; my flatmate had known I was going out to get the shelves, but it hadn't occurred to me to give her the address. We never did things like that.

Sitting there, I had a moment of sudden panic, as my imagination ran away with me. Was the sherry drugged? Was there some weird code I had missed in the wording of the ad, and had I turned up for some unspeakable expected sexual activity instead of the innocent purchase of a cheap set of bookshelves? Why had they shown me their bedroom?

Then Margaret asked me how I spelt my name. I spelt it for her.

'We never had a Rosita before,' she said, putting down the glass and reaching for something on a nearby table. It was a notebook. She opened it, and then flicked back through the pages. 'Oh,' she said. 'You're Irish. Perhaps you can tell us the correct spelling of an Irish name. A girl's name. I don't think we got it right, and we forgot to ask.' She spelled out 'E-e-f-a.'

I was staring hard at her by then. 'A-o-i-f-e,' I replied automatically, utterly confounded.

And then, their story emerged; a story they told with a degree of what I can only describe as merry fortitude. They had met each other late in life, when they were both retired, in the rural English town they lived in, whose unfamiliar name I forgot as soon as I heard it. Neither had been married before, nor had children, but they each owned a house. They lived for a few years in Margaret's house, and then decided to make another big life change.

'We always fancied living in London,' Henry said. 'The bright lights.'

'The shows,' Margaret said, her taffeta skirt rustling.

'City life. Something different. Something new,' Henry said.

Henry got up to refill our glasses. I stared down into the amber-coloured liquid, distractedly wondering how much sherry they got through a week. They seemed so jolly; a word that came unbidden into my head. They were so eager to be heard. I sat there, now pressed back into a corner of the sofa, listening, my hand carefully gripping the glass's bright, clear stem.

They told me they had sold both their houses and bought the one-bedroomed apartment in Primrose Hill. But life in London had not worked out the way they had thought it would.

'Bloody big city,' Henry said, matter-of-factly. 'Hard to get to know people. We don't even know our neighbours in this building.'

'We do go to shows,' Margaret said. 'We love the shows. But you can't attend the West End every night.'

They spoke with sunny, unembarrassed honesty of being aged newcomers to a big city, where they had no social networks; of the isolation of realizing they would be spending most days and nights on their own, three floors up in their mansion block. Underneath the cheeriness, the story of their loneliness in London gradually revealed itself, as shockingly intimate in its way, to me, the stranger, as the partially revealed pyjama leg under the pillow in their bedroom.

'And then we discovered *Loot*,' Margaret announced brightly. 'It's free to advertise. We had brought too much furniture with us, so we advertised to sell a table we didn't need.' They had offered free delivery with the table, and before long, their phone had rung.

'Sometimes we have as many as three people a week,' Henry said. 'We like it best when they come on Saturday, like you, because everyone has more time to talk then. It can be very rushed in the evenings, during the week. Everyone is usually so busy.'

'We got an answering machine,' Margaret said. 'In case anyone was ringing while we had popped out to the shops.'

'We don't do it every week,' Henry said. 'Every second week, usually. It's something to look forward to. We never know how many people will ring, you see. And of course, not all of them come to the flat.'

'It's not very good manners to say you're coming, and then you don't show up,' Margaret said. 'That happens sometimes.'

'We've got to see a lot of London, actually,' Henry said. 'Driving people around.'

There was a very large television in one corner of the room. Margaret indicated it with her outstretched sherry glass. 'We bought that with our earnings, if that's what you'd call them,' she said gaily. She pointed to other parts of the living room, reciting the names of the former items of its interior. The space was defined by its absences. 'There was a china cabinet that had belonged to my mother there,' she said, and I looked at the void on the wall behind me. 'Aoife, the one with the unusual Irish name, she bought the standard lamp that used to be at the end of the sofa. We didn't need it, and I was afraid Henry would trip over the flex.'

'Now, Margaret,' Henry reprimanded her, but he was smiling.

'It was a girl called Suzanne who bought that nice wooden towel rail we had. You know the kind, the upright ones, the old-fashioned ones,' she said.

'Yes,' I said.

'That was one of the first things we advertised. The bathroom here has a towel rail attached to the wall.'

'Where was it Suzanne was from again?' Henry asked.

Margaret consulted the notebook. 'Balham,' she said. 'Suzanne was from Balham. She was a social worker.' Balham was at the other side of London, south of the Thames. Suzanne had definitely been lured by the free transport.

'Can I please look at the notebook?' I asked, and Margaret handed it to me. The notebook had a picture of a bucolic garden on the cover, glowing with pink rose bushes. It was two-thirds full, with small, neat writing. Every entry was meticulously dated. The first date recorded was some eighteen months previously. Margaret wrote everyone's name down in the notebook, and what they had bought, and where they had come from, and what they did for a living.

'You have lovely handwriting,' I found myself saying. It seemed important just then to say something, no matter how inane.

'You do, don't you, Margaret?' Henry said proudly. 'I always said you had beautiful penmanship.'

I turned the pages of the notebook with fascination, imagining my own name in there by the end of the day. I wondered if Henry and Margaret disclosed their Chekhovian story to all their callers. Their clothes made sense to me now: I realized that they had dressed up specially for my visit; that I was their social occasion for the week.

'I must go,' I said eventually.

We carried the bookshelves into the lift, and went downstairs and put them into the back of their car. Then the three of us drove to Camden Town, Henry and Margaret continuing to ply me with yet more questions until we pulled up at Agar Place, and I got out with the shelves and waved them goodbye for ever.

I didn't go inside immediately. I stood there on the pavement for a while beside the shelves, thinking about what they might be saying to each other on the way back to their apartment, and going over the morning in my head again.

At the time, I was unsure whether to consider the experience creepy or sad, or both. It even haunted me for a while afterwards, as what I saw as a disturbing portent of the ageing process that lay ahead for me in decades to come; of possibly being alone and lonely. But now, I am not at all so sure that the experience was as sad as I automatically considered it to be when I was in my mid-twenties. Now, where I once saw only pathos in the couple, I see ingenuity and resourcefulness and an admirable ability to adapt to a new environment. Henry and Margaret had figured out a way to survive in a city where they knew no one, and they had seemed cheery about it.

Their story has stayed with me all these years. I pull it out like a worn pebble from a pocket, and turn it over at dinner parties, or late at night when drinking wine in someone's kitchen, or when I'm on a road trip. It always begins this way: 'Did I ever tell you the story about what happened when I lived in London and bought the bookshelves?'

Towards the end of that period in London, I lived in Lawford Road in Kentish Town with Miranda, an English girl my age, whom I knew through work. Our rooms at the top of an Edwardian house were rented out by Ethel, a very polite older lady who lived alone on the other two downstairs floors. Our landlady spent a lot of her time in the large back garden, wielding either secateurs or trowel, so that my most familiar sight of Ethel was the crown of her neat white head, which I frequently saw when I looked out of my bedroom window.

There was no door at the bottom of our flight of stairs to formally separate our floor from the rest of the house. The telephone was located in its own room off the downstairs hall, and the bell rang with a piercing volume and insistent ferocity at odds with the calm gentility of the rest of the house.

'If anyone asks, we are Ethel's great-nieces,' Miranda solemnly informed me. This was in case curious neighbours should ask any questions that might provoke interest from the taxman.

It was summer when I lived at Lawford Road, and our landlady's back garden was pulsing with roses. Every few days, either Miranda or I would discover morning offerings of just-cut blooms at the bottom of the stairs that led to our part of the house; deeply scented dark red, pink, and yellow old roses.

I read Bruce Chatwin for the first time that summer of the abundant roses. He had died the previous year of Aids, aged only forty-eight, although few people in 1989 were keen to publicly name the cause of his death. The politics of his death passed me by. I was just so sad that there would be no more books, because that summer, first *In Patagonia*, then *The Songlines*, and *What Am I Doing Here* entranced me; books I read with the windows open to the June sun, and the scent of roses everywhere in our little flat.

In Patagonia's opening lines stirred me in a way I couldn't explain.

'In my grandmother's dining-room, there was a glass-fronted cabinet and in that cabinet, a piece of skin. It was a small piece only, but thick and leathery, with strands of coarse, reddish hair. It was stuck to a card with a rusty pin. On the card was some writing in faded black ink, but I was too young then to read.

'What's that?'

'A piece of brontosaurus.'

I loved Chatwin's quest story; his travels in Patagonia to try and uncover the story behind the Giant Sloth that his grandmother's cousin, Charley Milward, had found in a cave in Patagonia in 1895. He had sold part of it to the British Museum (which is what the Natural History Museum was known as until 1922). Milward had also sent a fragment of skin to his cousin, Isobel, who named it as brontosaurus, and put it in her dining-room cabinet where it was to form the lodestone for her grandson's most famous book.

'Never in my life have I wanted anything as I wanted that piece of skin,' Chatwin wrote. I recognized that desire. I wanted what that storied piece of skin in his grandmother's cabinet represented, as much as Chatwin wanted to own it. It was redolent of adventures, travels, possibilities. I was twenty-four and wanted to experience all those things.

One Sunday, not long after I had read and reread *In Patagonia*, I went to the Natural History Museum in South Kensington. I lingered for a long time that afternoon in the Bird Gallery. One exhibit had drawn me to it: a peppermint-green painted Victorian cabinet of delicately stuffed hummingbirds. The cabinet contained scores of exquisite brightly coloured birds, their wings spread out like tiny jewelled fans. I had never seen a hummingbird before, alive or dead. The little label beside the cabinet read: 'They build their nests of spider webs and other very soft materials.' Within these miniature ethereal nests scattered artfully among the branches was the occasional white egg the size of a pinto bean. The wooden cabinet stood on wooden floorboards, and the vibrations created by people walking past made the dead hummingbirds' wings quiver slightly; an illusion of movement towards flight.

When I was finally ready to leave the Bird Gallery and the iridescent quivering cabinet, I kept indiscriminately wandering. There were meteorites; pieces from outer space that had fallen to Earth like reverse Icaruses. The unearthly piece of moon rock from the Taurus–Littrow Valley of the Moon, which Richard Nixon had presented to the people of England in the 1970s. There was the horror of a slab of melted glass and metal; bottles and drinking glasses and coins, all fused together, to show the intensity of the heat created by the Mount Pelée volcanic eruption of 8 May 1902, in Martinique. Of a town of 28,000 people, only two had survived.

And then, utterly by chance, the 'brontosaurus' skin. Late in the afternoon, I found myself in front of an unheralded cabinet that contained, right at the bottom, a piece of hide. It was on the cabinet's lowest shelf, flopped over partly on itself, a large piece of off-white hide and fur, like the bristly, thick coat of an unkempt Labrador dog. The label identified this exhibit as a piece of skin from an 'extinct giant ground sloth found in the Eberhardt Cave, Ultima Esperenza, Chile'.

I was electrified. It was thirteen years since *In Patagonia* had been published, but the label did not mention Chatwin's book, and although the museum was crowded, being a Sunday, nobody except myself was looking at this particular cabinet.

Was I really looking at the piece of skin that Charley Milward had sent to the British Museum from Chilean Patagonia; the same creature from which had come the fabled fragment of skin in Chatwin's grandmother's cabinet? Had this object been part of the tinder to the match of Chatwin's marvellous story? Had Chatwin once stood where I was, look-ing at what I was looking at? My excitement and curiosity tethered me to the cabinet until closing time: I simply could not stop staring at that piece of hide; its explanatory label almost concealed from view, so that if I had not stooped down to read it, I would have missed it altogether.

That evening, back at Lawford Road, I took out my Picador copy of *In Patagonia*, with its lovely turquoise and white cover where a ghost moon rose over the jagged Chilean mountains. I wanted to see what Chatwin had written about his visit to the South Kensington museum.

On the very first page of *In Patagonia*, Chatwin writes of a brontosaurus salvaged from the ice. Of how Charley Milward had this beast shipped to London, but the carcass spoiled en route, which is why visitors to the Natural History Museum saw bones, rather than skin. I read the page again. Bones, not skin? But I had seen only skin. There were definitely no bones in the cabinet; I had spent long enough looking into it that afternoon to be certain there were no bones. The text on the label, which I had written into my notebook, referred only to Giant Sloth skin, not bones.

On the following page, Chatwin writes that Milward's carcass was not the brontosaurus he fancied it to be, but a mylodon or Giant Sloth. That, in fact, he did not find an entire dead animal, or even a skeleton. He found some skin and bones, in a cave on Last Hope Sound in Chile. These he sent to England, where they were acquired by the British Museum. 'This version was less romantic but had the merit of being true.'

I put the book down, confused. It had to be the same piece of skin: the museum label had stated it was found in a cave at Ultima Esperanza, which was the Spanish for Last Hope; the place that Chatwin had himself given as the location of discovery. But why did he write that there were only bones on view in South Kensington, and not skin, when in fact, the reverse was true? *This version was less romantic but had the merit of being true.*

I searched through the rest of the book with the determination of a detective, but nowhere could I find any direct reference to Chatwin visiting the South Kensington museum. The only conclusion I could come to was that Bruce Chatwin had never actually bothered to visit the Natural History Museum in South Kensington to look at what remained of Milward's 'brontosaurus'. Yet he went to the other side of the world to seek out the place where it had originally been found. He went to the Natural History Museum in La Plata, near Buenos Aires, and saw there some of the same remains, 'and finally, I found some remains of the Giant Sloth, Mylodon Listai, from the cave of Last Hope Sound – claws, dung, bones with sinews attached, and a piece of skin.'

But why had he never gone to the place so close to his own home, in his own country? I could not stop puzzling over this. It would have been so easy to visit the London museum. Even if he had indeed sent the mythologized telegram of 1974 from New York to his *Sunday Times* editor – 'Gone to Patagonia for four months' – and thus left directly for Argentina, leaving no time for research in London, why had he not gone to South Kensington on his return? If he had, he would never have written that all you could see were bones, not skin.

Above all, I could not figure out why Chatwin would not have wanted to see for himself the remaining part of his heart's desire: the fragment in the cabinet had been lost; thrown out when his grandmother's house was sold in 1961. The skin was the origin object for his story, an object of which he had writ-ten: *Never in my life have I wanted anything as I wanted that piece of skin.* But he hadn't, actually, wanted to go and see what remained of that piece of skin. Why?

The previous December, I had found myself one Saturday in Camberwell, and realized I needed to find out the last posting dates abroad. With a stack of unmailed cards I ran into the post office there. Everyone else had had the same idea. The post office was buzzing and packed. There were so many of us waiting to be served that the queues for the var-ious counters took on snake-like shapes. I was busy writing the few last addresses on my pile of cards, balancing them awkwardly atop my bag, when I slowly became aware of a gradual silence.

It had been noisy with chat and laughter when I had arrived, and although there was still chatter going on, the vol-ume had decreased. I noticed people gathering their children to them, and the silence began to overtake the noise.

When I turned in the next loop of my particular snaking queue, I could see those waiting further back behind me. About ten people behind me was a woman, near whom nobody was standing. Or rather, the person directly behind her was keeping a distance of at least two places. Everyone was staring at this woman, and I found myself unable to stop staring too.

At first, I thought I was looking at someone dressed up as Santa Claus; there in the post office for the entertainment of the many small children. It was not someone dressed as Santa. It was a woman wearing all white. She had a wig of what looked like a Santa's beard; that thick, too-white, shiny acrylic stuff, which hung down in long, wholly unnatural hanks. She wore a white polo neck jumper, white gloves, a white pleated skater's skirt, white tights and white plimsolls. She carried a white bag. None of these white things were clean.

Her face was painted white, but not with make-up. It was painted in gloss house paint, the kind you use on domestic walls and need turpentine to remove splashes from wherever random spots land on your skin. There seemed to be several layers of it on her face, and some were cracking open, but many more remained beneath.

It was evident from the woman's bone structure and shape that she was black. It was like looking at the negative of a surreal photograph. She merely stared straight ahead, ignoring everyone, but I could not stop looking at her. I had all these questions roaring in my head. She had made a conscious decision when she got up in the morning to put on white clothes. But why? Who had painted her face? Had she done it herself? Why? Had she nobody to help her; nobody to tell her this was strange behaviour? Who was she? And what statement was she making by appearing to reverse the ethnicity of her skin colour in this way?

I reached the counter and paid for the stamps for my cards. I left the post office, but could not get the white woman who was not white out of my head. I went in for a coffee to a local café. The woman had seemed like a pariah, the way other people had stared at her. All I could think about was how vulnerable she must be. Or perhaps she simply felt terrible about her life and didn't care how she looked in public.

I too sometimes felt terrible about my life: that I was not being successful enough, or popular enough, and about the way I stupidly fell in love with men who did not love me back. I worried that I would never be able to write anything worth reading and that I was deluded in thinking I could be a writer. I wasn't interested in a career, because I didn't want to be tied down anywhere, and yet I fretted about the fact that I was unlikely ever to have one. I was afraid of the prospect of death, and of some day maybe losing my reason, and of not being alive any more, and even more afraid of the fact that these things were troubling me when I was only in my mid twenties. All these things made me feel truly dreadful from time to time. The fact was, bad as I sometimes felt, I could not imagine ever being in such mental distress that I went out in public looking as strange on the outside as I felt on the inside. But might I some day feel that bad? The woman I had just seen obviously felt terrible about something.

'I have just seen a woman all in white, but she's not white. In the post office. Just now,' I blurted out to the waitress. I felt I had to acknowledge her existence in some way.

The waitress knew who I meant. 'That one thinks she's an angel. That's why she dresses in white.'

'An angel?' I repeated stupidly.

A customer at another table joined in. 'I heard she dresses that way because she was raped by a white man. It's a protest.'

Yet another declared, 'She's the local nutcase. They let her out of the asylum last year.'

Angel. Rape survivor. Nutcase. I was young then and knew so little of life.

There are millions of people in London, and I encountered many of its representative disparate population from day to day in the years I lived there. Yet after all this time, it is Margaret and Henry in their Primrose Hill flat, and the nameless woman in Camberwell Post Office one December morning who have stayed with me ever since; who will always stay with me.

I had decided to go back to Ireland and spend three months hitch-hiking clockwise around the coast, with the intention of writing about it. I had realized at the end of my year in Australia that I knew it better than my own country, and I wanted to go and explore Ireland as if I was a stranger to it. The prospect of this self-imposed disruption to the life I had built in London scared and daunted and inspired me all at once.

Now I was working out my notice in my publishing job; a job I had held for scarcely a year. As I travelled back and forth each day from the office, I kept wondering if I was doing the right thing. I loved the Lawford Road flat. Miranda was an ever-surprising flatmate, with a legion of astonishing friends, who included me in their social events. I was having amazing experiences in London.

Was I being reckless, so swiftly leaving a career in a competitive profession that many people were trying to enter? I did like my job, but not enough to want to remain in it, when I could be doing more travelling instead. Yet I still fretted. Was I being foolish in choosing to leave England so soon, and the friends I had made there; leaving the whole, marvellous, inexhaustible city of London behind; a city that surprised me every day? I didn't know the answers to these questions. I only knew the compulsion to keep moving onwards, to do more, to see more; to feel the miles unspool beneath my feet, to answer the instinct that was driving me to keep on exploring; knew only that all this was too powerful to ignore.

It was Miranda who introduced me to what became one of my favourite places in London in those last months. She walked me one afternoon at lunchtime to the atmospheric run-down Museum of Garden History in the grounds of St Mary-at-Lambeth Church in Vauxhall. It was presided over by older ladies who, I suspected, were dedicated gardeners, and even in summer, the church was chilly. There were various vintage gardening tools on display, but the true attraction of the place were the tombs that stood in the piece of walled garden that still remained behind the church.

The garden held the tomb of William Bligh, and also the fantastical high slab of stone that commemorates John Tradescant the Elder, and his son, also named John Tradescant. Miranda walked me around it that first time, pointing out the crocodiles, the wild, exotic carvings of many-headed sea monsters, the Middle-Eastern-looking classical ruins; all so much at odds with the thoroughly urban London traffic that hummed on the other side of the churchyard wall.

'The Tradescants were explorers and gardeners,' Miranda explained. They were like old friends to her, she knew so much about their lives. I had never heard of them before. They had collected seeds and bulbs on their travels in the seventeenth century, bringing them back to the gardens of royalty and aristocracy in England. Moreover, John Tradescant the Elder had also brought back a collection of strange and exotic objects. He had the eye of both magpie and voyeur, of curator, and practitioner of ethnography.

I went back several times, to eat my lunchtime sandwiches and circumnavigate the astounding tomb. From one of the ladies, I bought a copy of the Tradescants' epitaph, carved on the surface of the enormous tomb.

Know, stranger, ere thou pass, beneath this stone
Lie John Tradescant grandsire, father, son
The last died in his spring, the other two
Lived till they had travelled orb and nature thro'
As by their choice collections may appear
Of what is rare in land, in sea, in air
Whilst they (as Homer's Iliad in a nut)
A world of wonders in one closet shut
These famous Antiquarians that had been
Both gardeners to the Rose and Lily Queen
Transplanted now themselves, sleep here and when
Angels shall with their trumpets waken men
And fire shall purge the world, these three shall rise
And change this garden then for a Paradise.

A world of wonders in one closet shut. Long before Chatwin was entranced by the piece of 'brontosaurus' skin in his grandmother's cabinet, other people were creating their own cabinets of curiosities. This is what John Tradescant the Elder created with the objects he brought back with him; objects connected only by their marvellous singularity. For a time they were held in his house in Lambeth, London, and are now held in the Ashmolean Museum in Oxford.

Later, I found a list of some of the objects in the collection, as recorded by a man called Georg Christoph Stirn in 1638.

'In the museum of Mr John Tradescant, are the following things . . . a salamander, a chameleon, a pelican, a remora, a lanhado from Africa, a white partridge, a goose which has grown in Scotland on a tree, a flying squirrel, another squirrel like a fish, all kinds of bright coloured birds from India, a number of things changed into stone . . . the hand of a mermaid, the hand of a mummy, a very natural wax hand under glass, all kinds of precious stones, a picture wrought in feathers, a small piece of wood from the cross of Christ . . . a cup of an E Indian alcedo which is a kind of unicorn, many Turkish and other foreign shoes and boots, a sea parrot, a toad-fish, an elk's hoof with three claws, a bat as large as a pigeon . . . Indian arrows such are used by the executioners in the West Indies – when a man is condemned to death, they lay open his back with them and he dies of it . . . a few goblets of agate, the passion of Christ carved very daintily on a plumstone . . . a scourge with which Charles V is said to have scourged himself, a hat band of snake bones.'

I remain fascinated by lists like these; of seemingly unrelated things. *The hand of a mermaid, a few goblets of agate, a hat band of snake bones.* It was only later, when I made my own ad hoc dictionary, that I realized this random collection of words was, in its own way, a kind of literary cabinet of curiosities. And only much later again did I realize that the cumulative experiences of travelling are akin to creating your own Wunderkammer, which you can perpetually curate afterwards in your memory.

Perhaps this is what Bruce Chatwin did, when he sat down to write *In Patagonia,* and what all writers do. There is always reddish hair and ghosts of bones and heart's desires, all jumbled together to create our own particular mythologies.

Pakistan
1995

BRAME

- fierce longing,
passion

BY THE TIME I got to Pakistan, in April 1995, I had been on many local Asian buses. My travels on this journey had started the previous October, in Nepal. I was making my way slowly back overland to Europe; a journey that would eventually take eight months. I had been on Nepalese buses whose roofs were so overloaded with people and goods that they sometimes shed both passengers and cargo going round corners (twice, I saw people falling past the window; multiple times, baggage); on Indian buses that bizarrely drove kamikaze at night without headlights (to save battery power, I was told); and on buses in both countries that broke down in the middle of nowhere, where we waited many, many hours for the wounded vehicle to be patched up. I had learned that in the same way that silence is part of a conversation, patience is part of the rhythm of travelling. I had also learned to fear the authentically colourful local bus.

The minibus that brought me to Gilgit from Rawalpindi was a journey scheduled to take fourteen hours. On this journey, I was sitting up front, in the prized minibus spot alongside the driver, where Western women, whenever there were any, were given a seat. It was prized because it was the only place in the bus where you did not have to share your seat with another person: every bus I ever took in Asia had many more passengers than seats. There were no other female tourists on the bus with me on this journey; indeed, no back-packers at all.

The bus left Rawalpindi an hour and a half late; an entirely routine delay. There were, as I had become accustomed to on long-distance journeys, two drivers. Their names were Zahoor and Saleem. Saleem was driving as we left Rawalpindi; Zahoor between us. They were Gilgit men, thin under the folds of their shalwar kameez, curious, as everyone in Asia was, as to why I was travelling alone.

'Why you travel alone?' Zahoor enquired. 'Where your husband?'

'My husband is dead,' I said, matter-of-factly. My erst-while husband had died many different deaths by then; fanciful deaths I enjoyed inventing. 'He drowned while deep-sea fishing in Sri Lanka,' I said on this occasion. In the past few months, he had, variously, been accidentally shot in a jungle in Borneo, died in a plane crash in the Sahara desert, been bit-ten by a snake in Cambodia, fallen from a cliff in Venezuela, and succumbed to altitude sickness in Nepal.

My husband was not always dead. Sometimes I resurrected him. If someone – always a male someone – was too pushy, too smarmy, or too keen to be tactile, on those occasions, my hus-band lived and breathed, and was eagerly awaiting me back at the guesthouse, or in the next town, or at that tea-house just over there. I had a ring purchased from a Kathmandu bazaar, which I wore on my wedding finger. The truth was just too confounding a cultural chasm for the people I met along the way: that I was in fact a woman travelling alone at the age of twenty-nine out of choice.

The other truth was that I was in love with a man I had met briefly in the unlikely circumstances of a funeral in Edinburgh, not long before I left to go travelling. He was standing in front of me in the church, a tall still man, with long black hair, which I vaguely registered, while listening to the hymns.

Back at the funeral lunch in the family home, I caught sight of him again, and this time saw his face. He had that accidental fortune of high cheekbones and underlying facial bone structure that you know a person will carry with them their life through, like the classic profile that endures on a struck medal or coin.

His eyes were an unusual shade of blue, almost navy. With his long hair, and height, he stood out among the sombre black suits in the room; carrying a wholly different kind of energy to everyone else there. We eventually found ourselves standing nearby in the large room, balancing our cups of coffee, staring openly at each other. Among the polite shuffling and reaching of mourners for sandwiches and plates and cups, at some point, we found ourselves right beside each other.

'Alan was my PhD supervisor,' he said, by way of introduction. 'I'm Jake.'

I told him my name. 'Alan was the father of my friend Alexander,' I said, indicating my friend across the room.

'You're Irish,' Jake said, catching the accent. 'Do you live in Edinburgh?'

'London. I came up on the train yesterday. I'm going back this afternoon.' I could smell his cologne; something unusual I couldn't identify; something I knew I would always remember. I had a sudden urge to reach up and touch his cheek. The cup rattled on the saucer in my hand. We talked for a while about the man whose funeral it had been.

Then Jake said, 'Let me walk you back to Waverley, whenever you're going.'

'I was thinking of heading off now. Let me just say good-bye to Alex and the others.' I hugged half a dozen people, retrieved my bag from the hall, and stepped under the crook of Jake's arm as he held the front door open for me. We walked.

'This is going to sound a bit mad, but would you like to stop for a drink?' Jake asked. We were on Elm Row, outside the Windsor Bar. It was mid-afternoon.

'Sure,' I said, although I was not sure at all. I had no idea what was happening.

In the Windsor Bar, where we were almost the only customers, we talked for hours. About our lives. About our ambitions. About everything. He was completing a doctorate in physics; a subject I knew nothing about. He unselfconsciously used words like jurisprudence and lodestone; words that I had to ask him to define for me. Usually I was the one with the armoury of words. We were wholly focused on each other. We could not get our respective stories out fast enough. We kept going down more roads of conversation; travelling deeper and deeper into some new shared, yet unexplored terrain. How can it be this easy? I thought, shocked.

It wasn't. Eventually, Jake spoke the one word that made me feel foolish: 'girlfriend'. I didn't even grasp the sentence, just the word, which landed like a blow to my solar plexus. I excused myself as soon as decently possible and went to the Ladies. In the bathroom, I leaned against the stall door with my eyes closed and scolded myself for feeling so disproportionally disappointed; so suddenly bereft of a person I had only just met. He had a girlfriend. Of course he did. How could I not have picked up on it earlier? But how was I to know, until he told me?

'I must go catch my train,' I said with fake cheeriness, when I went back outside. We were not quite finished our drinks, but I didn't feel like sitting down again.

Jake was disconcerted. 'Are you sure?'

En route to the station from the bar, we didn't talk. There was everything and nothing to say. Then Jake stopped walking, and so did I. He simply held his arms out, and I cast myself directly into them. We kissed for a long time; in full view on the street, urgent and uncaring. I was rarely so physically intimate in public, and somehow sensed Jake was not either, but it had been impossible to walk another step in silence without trying to continue the conversation by touch instead.

I could scarcely breathe, and it was nothing to do with the fact that we were gripping each other so hard. To me, our embrace felt so familiar, so right, and also somehow so perilous. We stood there together on the street, holding each other tightly, breathing hard, not moving.

At Waverley Station, we discovered that I had missed not just my original train, but every train that day to London. It was a bank holiday, and the schedule had been truncated. I had not thought to check what time the last trains left, as I had confidently planned to be gone from Scotland by the late afternoon.

Jake and I looked at each other carefully on the concourse. 'You could stay at my place,' he said.

'I could,' I said, guardedly. I could not believe I had missed every train back to London. I never missed trains. It seemed that we were destined to spend more time together, although I didn't believe in fate, or destiny or any of those things.

We went to another bar, and kept talking, but for me, a large part of the joy at our unexpected connection had leached away. At Jake's place, which he shared with flatmates, there was no one else home. I did not ask about the whereabouts of the girlfriend. The light had faded from the day, and he didn't turn on any lamps. We had stopped talking. We kissed again for a long time as the darkness bloomed, and then I pushed him away. Or he stopped. Or we heard someone open the apartment door, out in the hall. It was very late, not long off an early dawn. Eventually, Jake went to his room.

I spent what remained of the night on a pile of cushions on the living-room floor; sleepless and fully dressed. The day had felt like a week, a century, a second. I couldn't process what had happened, or what I was feeling, except it felt momentous, and terrifying.

Some time before 7 a.m., I got up, intending to let myself out. Before leaving me the previous night, Jake had drunkenly asked if I would write down my phone number and address, and I had drunkenly promised I would do it in the morning, but when sobriety and morning came, I did not. Although I was moving as quietly as I could, Jake emerged from his room as I was about to open the apartment door.

'You're going,' he said bluntly. 'Please don't go yet.'

I stared at him. I longed to cross the space and continue all our conversations, but I could not. 'I'm going,' I said with determination, and pulled the door out after me, much harder and louder than I had intended. On the train back to London, a faint scent of that cologne exuded from me; from my skin or clothes, I couldn't tell. By the time I had crossed London and reached the house on Coldharbour Lane, it had dissipated.

Some weeks later, when again about to use the daypack I'd brought to Edinburgh, I found Jake's card right at the bottom. He must have dropped it in there without me noticing, I realized; perhaps when I had gone to the bathroom. Jolted, I held the small white piece of cardboard in my hand and looked at it. I had gone over our meeting many times in my head in the intervening weeks. I remembered the way his lips had felt on my neck. I remembered the way he had made me feel when we talked; as if we had known each other always, and always would. I remembered how we had looked at each other when the station guard had told us the last trains to London had left.

I stood for a long time in my bedroom, staring at the card, turning it over and over in my hand. It felt like a dangerous second chance. I was afraid, but also so curious about what might happen if we met again. Suddenly full of longing, I decided that I would write Jake a card and send the contact details I had not left behind me in Edinburgh. It would be up to him then.

The next day, I sent a postcard to the address on the card, and waited. I had sent the phone number of our communal landline in the hall. Every time it rang, I jumped, and my heart lurched. I avoided answering it. Two days after I had sent the card, I was in the kitchen making dinner when the phone rang again. One of my housemates answered.

'Rosita!' he called. 'It's for you.'

I held the receiver to my ear as if it was a seashell and I was listening for the sound of the ocean deep within it. 'Hello,' I said, my heart thudding as I heard Jake's laughing voice again.

There had been a second, longer rendezvous shortly after, in London. I went to meet his train at King's Cross. At the station, Jake was wearing a black leather jacket, and his hair was loose. I saw him on the platform just before he saw me, and he looked both joyous and nervous, and then, when he spotted me, wholly joyous.

'You came,' he said, hugging me fiercely. 'I wasn't sure if you would.'

'I'm here,' I said, while the crowds pushed and shoved their way past us, standing still as one in the moving throng;

a steadfast rock in a moiling ocean. When we started walking to the Tube, he put his arm around my shoulder, and I put mine around his waist. We did not break the perfect pace we at once discovered.

'Look how well we fit together,' Jake said.

'Yes.'

Nobody slept on the living-room floor that night. I did not push him away. We lay on my bed and held on to each other as if the bed was a lifeboat, and the floor beneath an ocean of unknown depths and dangers. We did not sleep much.

When did I fall in love with him? When he stood beside me first, radiating that physicality that had made me want to touch his face? When I realized he could summon words that I could not? When I felt that he was already so familiar to me? When he had kissed the nape of my neck, and I knew I had never felt so alive in my life? When we were fiercely tangled up together in my bed, like a knot that would never come undone?

If I spoke of love, would you bid me be silent? Jake wrote to me, in a long letter from Edinburgh that crossed with my own. *You seemed so full of light, so blazing. I never knew such light.* I read the letter over and over. I had never known words could be such dangerous things.

Soon after I got that letter, less than a month after Jake had come to London, I walked into Trailfinders in Covent Garden and impulsively bought a one-way ticket to Kathmandu in Nepal. The ticket was for a mere few weeks hence. Before meeting Jake, I had already planned to travel for several months in central Asia at some point in the near future but, until that day, hadn't decided when to start. I couldn't stay still. I knew being in love with a man who was already in a partnership with someone else was a hopeless challenge I didn't want. So I did what I always did in those situations: I made plans to leave before I was the one who was left.

I had already made my decision: Jake was the person I wanted to be with, in whatever lay ahead. I knew I could no more not have loved Jake than I could have stopped breathing; he had become part of whatever constituted my soul, if such an entity exists. I think it does. It seemed so obvious to me that we had each unexpectedly found something extraordinary in the other, but it was up to Jake to figure out his own complicated personal situation. I knew I couldn't bear to be on the same land mass as him, as he agonized about what to do; the train tracks to Scotland called to me every time I found myself at King's Cross and caught sight of the destination boards.

If I had a non-refundable airline ticket, I reasoned, it meant I had to leave England, and in my febrile state of mind at that time, I thought that was the best thing to do. I had never been so simultaneously confused yet so sure of anything in my life. I had never been so happy, and so unhappy.

Meanwhile, until I left, the devastatingly articulate letters from Edinburgh continued to arrive, and the phone of the house where I lived in Brixton continued to ring with calls from Scotland.

In those days, there were no internet cafés, no mobile phones, no Skype and no social media. In Asia, my letters arrived via poste restante, or at American Express offices, and it took hours to connect to an outside line in expensive offices that existed solely for phone calls. In Delhi the previous month, I had stayed in my guesthouse for an entire day and a half, awaiting a possible phone call from Jake, which came in the half-hour I ran out for lunch on the second day: I had sent the number in a letter with travellers who were returning to England and had promised to post it as soon as they landed. In that whole journey of eight months, Jake and I never once spoke on the phone.

As I travelled onwards, at each infrequent mail drop at American Express there were piles of letters from Jake. I wrote to him frequently, sometimes pressing my letters into the hands of fellow travellers I called carrier pigeons, who were soon returning to Britain. His ever-growing pile of letters to me was tied in a length of red ribbon I had bought in a drapery in Darjeeling. I read and reread his letters, as he did mine. I had no idea what I was going to do on return to Europe, but I hoped my travels would give me some clarity and resolution of mind before returning – and do the same for Jake.

And now here I was in Pakistan some six months into my journey. After the mountains, my plan was to cross the country by train, to Quetta, and then travel onwards to the border crossing with Iran, at Taftan.

'I am sorry, sister,' Zahoor said, as he digested the loss of my drowned husband. In Pakistan, all the men called me their sister. I collected brothers every day.

It was very hot, and soon I fell asleep while watching the unlovely suburbs of Rawalpindi disappear into the dusk. The road runs for over 1,300 kilometres, from north of Rawalpindi over the Khunjerab Pass into China, and ends (or begins) in Kashgar. It shadows the ancient Silk Road trading route; a name resonant with exploration, commerce and adventure. Some hours later, we passed through Abbottabad, a city whose name, almost exactly sixteen years later, was to become infamous around the world as the place where Osama bin Laden was discovered.

The road climbed steadily upwards, into the mountains. In the Karakoram mountain range, the road reaches an elevation of over 4,500 metres. Some time around midnight I awoke, and found myself the only person in the bus. In the distance, a fire glowed within a hut. Far below us, a river glittered palely in the moonlight, and all around, the mountains made their own darkness in the night.

When I got out of the bus, I shivered. We were high up now, where the air was sharp, carried off glaciers in gusts like a series of flying knives. After the heat and dust of the lowlands and the city, with its smells of exhaust and dirt, of burning rubbish and cooking oil and human shit, the mountain air was shocking. It smelt cold and wild and strange, and I loved it.

'Sister!' Saleem called, beckoning me to the shack. I was placed beside the fire, and handed first a bowl of chai and then a plate of dahl. The rotis spun hot from the griddle like flying saucers. I ate several.

'Good?' Saleem enquired.

'Very good,' I said, devouring them, aware as I did that neither of them were eating. Saleem was rolling joints, passing them to other men around the fire, and also, I noticed, to Zahoor, whose turn to drive it was probably going to be after this rest stop.

'Do you change drivers here now?' I asked, also noticing that Saleem, having distributed several joints, was now smoking one himself. We'd left Rawalpindi more than six hours previously. So far, Saleem had done all the driving.

Saleem laughed, and gave Zahoor a dig in the ribs. For the first time, I noticed that Zahoor was holding his left hand in the sleeve of his shalwar. He saw me looking, pulled his hand from his sleeve and held it out for my inspection. The hand, in a bandage, fell down at a curious, unnatural angle from the wrist. He was also shivering, and looked feverish in a way he had not when we had departed Rawalpindi. 'Hand is broke,' he announced simply, and allowed Saleem to feed him a number of what I assumed were antibiotics – but who knew what they were – from a silver card in his pocket.

'Hand is broke,' I repeated stupidly. 'And you are driver?'

'Problem, problem,' Zahoor incanted mournfully, continuing to shiver, a large joint in his one good hand.

I have never been good at maths, but even my abysmal algebra was up to this problem. There were two men, Saleem and Zahoor, who were to share the driving for fourteen hours. Before we started, there had been a delay of ninety minutes. Zahoor, who has a broken wrist and is now smoking a joint, is no longer part of the driving equation. Does Saleem, who has already driven for six hours, and is now also smoking a joint, continue to drive the remaining number of hours, whatever they may be, all without sleep, on a mountain road to Gilgit?

We got back on the bus. The drivers giggled like boys, and decided to conduct an experiment. Zahoor, limp hand inside his shalwar like a left-handed Nelson, got in the driver's seat. Saleem rode shotgun alongside him, to act as a substitute for Zahoor's broken left hand in changing the gears. This lasted a jumpy, laughing mile or so, while we swerved and careered along the dark road. I was terrified, but didn't want to chide them, as I was afraid it might make them even more reckless.

They swapped back again, and it was Saleem who remained in the driver's seat after that. The further north we drove along the Karakoram Highway, the more frequent the army checkpoints. They were all the same: a random bamboo pole across the road, charpoys (the ubiquitous string and bamboo beds of

Asia) alongside them, where soldiers not on duty lay snoring wrapped in blankets. 'We Stay Awake So The Country Can Sleep' declared the sign at every checkpoint.

I had to get off the bus at every checkpoint, go into the hut and write my name, address, occupation, passport number and onward destination in two, sometimes three, thick ledgers. For occupation, I put 'writer', although I had no idea what I really was. I had published two books by then; one a collection of poetry and the other a non-fiction book about spending a winter hitch-hiking the coast of Ireland. The second book had received an award in the form of a substantial bursary in literature from the Irish Arts Council; money I had then used to fund a seven-month ad hoc journey in and around Eastern Europe and Turkey.

My last job in London had been as a researcher for a survey company. They were doing pre-survey work on a questionnaire for customers of a famous fast-food restaurant as to whether they would be interested or not in being offered healthy salad options, along with fries and burgers. In those days before Google, part of the research involved spending days in the British Library Newspaper Archive at Colindale in north London. Most of my work consisted of writing up our findings; something I found easy, although the merits of salad versus burgers was a subject with limited scope.

The Pakistani soldiers thumbed through my passport. They scowled at my Indian visa; relations between the two countries could hardly be worse. 'India no good! Why you waste time in India?' they asked belligerently. 'Pakistan is better, yes?'

'Pakistan is a very beautiful country,' I answered diplomatically, although by that point, all I had seen of it were Lahore and the twin cities of Rawalpindi and Islamabad, none of which I had found in the slightest bit beautiful. The soldiers handed me back my passport with a flourish, smiled, and called me their sister.

The journey from Rawalpindi to Gilgit took a total of twenty-two hours, and after the failed experiment with the gearstick, Saleem drove the whole way. The time included another rest stop at another mountainside shack, and a further unscheduled stop while a party of road-workers partially cleared a recent rockfall, so that we could continue by driving over the most manageable pile of rocks. Zahoor's primary function on the trip, as far as I could make out, was to continue to roll joints one-handedly for Saleem. With his broken wrist, he could never have been coming along as a relief driver, although again, who knew? I was looking at it through a Western lens as usual, and not seeing how it really was, however that might be.

We finally drove into Gilgit some time after four in the afternoon. Saleem sounded the horn triumphantly and then lay across the steering wheel in exhaustion. By then, Zahoor was asleep on the floor under my feet, his head pillowed on my daypack. There were maybe ten or fifteen seconds after arriving in Gilgit when nobody stirred, as if we were all adjusting to the fact that we had actually, really arrived.

Then Zahoor woke, and clambered up on to the seat beside me, Saleem lifted his head from the steering wheel, and they chorused as one, 'Sister, welcome to Gilgit!'

The Madina Hotel, at the end of a nondescript laneway off Northern Light Infantry Chowk, was flanked by tall walls. The heavy brown wooden door was camouflaged in the brown wall, snug as tongue in groove. There was no handle. I put my palm against the door and it swung open quietly.

Afterwards, when I thought of the Madina, where I stayed for several days, it seemed as if the noise of the town stopped at its door. Gilgit was all noise: horns honking, cocks crowing, the poetic wail of the muezzin from the minarets, the busyness of the bazaar, the rattling of cauldrons at street-front restaurants and chai stalls, old men spitting in the street. Within the high walls of the Madina, all was peace.

Small tables and white-painted chairs were set under apricot trees that distributed their scented petals at random; on to my open diary, a cup of green tea, my hair. There was a bright square of lawn and a vegetable garden. The mountains cast their shadows on the far walls of the garden each afternoon. The rooms lay in small, scattered one-storey blocks that overlooked the garden.

Muhammad Yaqoob, the hotel's owner, had sleepy brown eyes and a large round smile. He had the deceptive physical smallness of all the northern Pakistani men, which belied their strength and ability; they could lift loads I could scarcely imagine any man handling. Muhammad barely reached to my shoulder. He showed me to my room, at the far end of the garden. It was large and dim, with a corrugated iron roof, two single beds, a fan, a metal desk and one chair.

'Your husband?'

'Dead,' I replied automatically, too weary to invent another imaginative death. It had been five days since I had crossed by rickshaw the border from Amritsar in India towards Lahore, and I had been travelling four of those five days. It was still late afternoon, but all I wanted to do was lie down on one of those beds and sleep.

By the time I woke up, some time after eight that evening, the power was off, and the silence was absolute. I was to learn that three nights out of four Gilgit surrendered to darkness. 'Load shedding' was the term everywhere for the fact that there was not enough of an electricity supply to match the demand. Some of the guesthouses and hotels I had stayed in had generators that roared like troubled lions all night, for the sake of a tepid shower and a very low wattage light in your room. The Madina was not one of them, and I was glad: the darkness had a kind of relentless honesty to it that appealed to me.

It was like being underground in Gilgit when the sun went down and the power failed. Candles and paraffin lamps burned random holes in the labyrinthine streets of the bazaar, which I walked through by torchlight. The men crouched over their candlelit tin plates in filthy restaurants looked like subjects in a Rembrandt painting. The radios were silent, the televisions, always tuned to cricket, went unseen, music from the occasional ghetto blaster went unplayed. The silence and darkness were almost medieval. Gilgit had telephones, a plane service and a road that went to China. Yet three nights out of four, the town seemed to travel back in time.

It was mostly a one-storey town, all flat roofs and open-sided wooden shacks. Mountains balanced on the roofs, and where we were, up so high, it seemed as if the sky was merely a canopy, stretched between peaks. Evidence of trade with China was everywhere in the bazaar. There were pictures of blood-red sunsets, and machine-embroidered wall hangings in velvet and gold thread, of pagodas and birds that looked like none I knew. There were bunches of plastic flowers, battery-operated clocks with hands made of butterfly wings, storks carved from cork under domes of glass, slippers embroidered with peevish-looking dogs and 99-piece tea sets in pink, yellow or green.

Tourism, particularly Chinese tourism, was evidently expected to develop greatly in the near future: on our way into Gilgit I had seen the raw construction of several big new hotels along the Karakoram Highway. When I was there, the Madina was about as fancy as accommodation got.

I bought candles in the bazaar and stayed up on load-shedding evenings, reading, or writing letters or in my diary by their light. One of these evenings I sat in the tiny lobby with Muhammad and some of his friends, all dismayed that the power had gone off during a crucial televised cricket match, although it seemed to me that every cricket match was a crucial one in Pakistan. We drank green tea by candlelight.

The Khunjerab Pass on the Karakoram Highway, which was the border crossing between Pakistan and China, did not open to foreigners until 1 May. It was only the first week of April. As a result, there were few backpackers up this far north. I was the only guest in the Madina that evening, as I had been on most evenings. One night, there had been four Japanese men and an English couple, and the previous evening, an Australian man, but tonight, I was the only guest again. The silt of darkness lay everywhere. On the rest of this journey, in Nepal and India and Sri Lanka, I had rarely been without the easy friendship of other backpackers; had hardly ever eaten dinner alone or lacked company and conversation. In Gilgit, apart from my daily circumnavigation of the bazaar and the chats with Muhammad, I was spending a lot of time alone.

'Muhammad,' I said. 'If any other people arrive, can you please put them in a room on my side of the garden? It gets a bit lonely over there.'

Muhammad roared with laughter. His cricket-mad friends looked at him with alarm. His eyes closed fully. He clapped his hands together with mirth. Chuff-chuff-chuff, he went. His shoulders shook. At last he drew breath. 'Rosita, you are crazy woman!' he spluttered. 'You tell me you go to the Iran by yourself when you leave Pakistan, but you are lonely in my nice hotel in Gilgit, yes? Rosita, I would not go to the Iran by myself.' Muhammad was dead amused at my priorities.

At any rate, when I went to my room that night, I discovered one of the kitchen boys had taken his charpoy and set it up under my window; sent there by Muhammad to protect me from my fears, imagined or otherwise. I sat up late, reading by candlelight, and drinking the illicit firewater Red Dragon Chinese whisky Muhammad had procured for me a few days earlier. I could hear the gentle snores of the kitchen boy on the other side of the wall.

At dawn, I heard him stirring, and looked out the window. Like Lazarus, he arose, picked up his bed, and simply walked away.

The map of the Karakoram I had bought in Muhammad Beg's book stall in the bazaar was spread out in front of me on one of the tables in the garden of the Madina. It was a large, laminated hand-drawn map in black and white. 'Trekking and Mountaineering Map,' it declared. 'Karakoram: Gilgit, Hunza, Rakaposhi, Batura area.'

The map's symbols were explained in a reference key at the bottom. Their meanings thrilled me: glaciers, mule tracks, monasteries, cave shelters, unmetalled roads, unfrequented tracks, and heights. Heights there definitely were: clusters of peaks just in this one region alone of over 6,000 metres.

The heights and mountains were inked in thick black, and in between the mountains bulged odd shapes that I initially thought were pools or lakes, indicated by broken lines. They were neither pools nor lakes, they were glaciers. The Pakistanis called their glaciers 'Ice Dragons', and the northern region where I was had the densest concentration beyond the Poles. The Batura Glacier, which swung across the map like a meandering river, was 58 kilometres long.

The Karakoram Highway itself was not easy to distinguish, overwhelmed as it was by the vastness of the natural phenomena all around. The villages it passed through were tiny black scratches. The hand-drawn map, it was clear to me, was merely an impression of a landscape and its topography; hints of what lay beyond Gilgit. No serious trekker, let alone mountaineer, would ever put their trust in such a map. But I figured it would be fine for my purposes, because my intention was simply to walk north along the Karakoram Highway from Gilgit to the village of Karimabad in the Hunza Valley. Depending on which map or piece of literature I was currently looking at, the distance between the two was 40 miles, 52 miles, or 60 miles. I estimated it would take me three days.

According to my new map, there was a Government Rest House at Nilt, the second village en route. I had read about these rest houses in my guidebook. A network of bungalows scattered around the country, they'd been built to accommodate visiting government agents and were available to tourists if not in use.

As to accommodation at the first overnight village, Rahimabad, there was no solid information, but when I asked in the bazaar I was told there was a small local hotel. I wanted to walk along the Karakoram Highway for many reasons. Mostly because it shadowed the ancient Silk Road, and for centuries people had travelled it on foot, with mules and yaks. I was no explorer or adventurer, but I wanted to add my footsteps to those who had gone before me; and to see the same astonishing mountain ranges. Walking meant I'd have time to properly see the landscape I was moving through; to get a better scale of its mighty immensity. I also wanted a break from the local bus. I was sure I could make Rahimabad well before nightfall the next day if I left early that morning. I had already been to the bazaar to pick up what few provisions I could find there: dried apricots, nuts and a bag of little macaroons so hard they bounced when I let one fall by accident. And I had a bottle of iodine in my rucksack, which I used for purifying water.

Muhammad came over to see what it was I was looking at. I told him of my plans. He frowned. 'No, this is not good,' he said. 'You are one person only.' This was indisputable. But all I wanted to do was walk along a clearly marked road in full daylight. It was hardly the stuff of wild adventures. It was true that the little tourist leaflets I had picked up along the way warned vigorously against travelling at night on this stretch of the Karakoram Highway, and of camping in remote or secluded places, but I had no intention of doing either of those things. 'There is a nice bus,' Muhammad offered. 'Going Karimabad every day from Gilgit.'

'I don't want to go on a bus,' I said stubbornly. 'I want to walk to Karimabad.'

'But you are only one! And you are woman!' Muhammad tapped the map in agitation. He pointed to areas off the road between Gilgit and Rahimabad, between Rahimabad and Nilt. 'There are bandits!' he hissed.

I looked down at the map again, this time a little more uneasily. 'How do you know?'

'Because they are always stopping the lorries on the road and stealing their cargo. At night, the buses and lorries, they do not travel alone. They go together, in convoy. It is safer this way. If the bandits see you walking, they will follow you. Rob you. Maybe other things too. These are bad men!' He was gesticulating with urgency.

I put away the map for a while. I always listened to local advice, and almost always heeded it, but I had heard nothing from anyone else about bandits in this part of the country. I did not want to give myself an excuse not to do this. Something stubborn in me wanted to walk on the Karakoram Highway. I had hitch-hiked huge distances by myself for months all around Australia, and then for three months around the coast of Ireland. I had learned to be streetwise, and I had kept myself safe by carefully judging risks: did this driver seem overly sleazy as he rolled down the window (almost 99 per cent of my lifts were with solitary male drivers), or did that one have a smell of alcohol on his breath, or why was it that particular one made me feel uneasy and thus refuse the lift? Of course every country and situation was different, but I honestly did not believe I would be putting myself in any real danger by walking for a couple of days along the Karakoram Highway. I decided I would take the risk.

By 8 a.m. the next morning, I was walking along the Karakoram Highway carrying just my daypack, having left my rucksack at the Madina.

'I'll be back in about a week,' I had said to Muhammad, who had silently taken my rucksack and shoved it into a cupboard off the lobby without looking me in the eye.

It was a chill morning, and I strode along, putting the tiny village of Dainyor behind in a couple of hours. I passed orchards of apricots, their white petals a nimbus around each tree. The Hunza River was on my left; a pale green colour. Everything else in the landscape was grey, black or white. I had been mistaken in thinking the Karakoram Highway would be a tranquil place. It was a ferocious landscape. I was walking between mountains, on a ledge some 100 metres above the river. Down the sides of the mountains ran rivers of scree, fanning out towards the bottom of the valley floor. Behind and between the mountains lay glaciers, and on top of those lay snow. Snow and ice, endlessly nudging away at rock and shale and stone. The further I walked, the more I began to feel the landscape was balancing precariously above me.

Some time after 4 p.m., I arrived at Rahimabad. My *Lonely Planet Pakistan* did not have an entry on it. It was the tiniest of villages, bisected neatly by the road. A few scattered houses, a handful of shop-shacks and a chai stall on one side, and on the other, a one-storey wooden building with a painted sign outside that said 'Hotel'. Kids stood bug-eyed in doorways, staring as I walked down the street. The men at the chai stall looked up, startled, from their game of Ludo. I had been fascinated to see the popularity of Ludo in Gilgit. Men at chai stalls in the bazaar there played draughts too, but it was games of Ludo I saw most often.

This cardboard Ludo board on the ground outside the chai stall at Rahimabad, like many of the others I had seen, was so worn that the colours had all but vanished from its paper surface. Sure-handed players moved their counters on invisible squares, the original layout of the board still a clear memory in their heads.

The building that advertised itself as a hotel was a long, windowless structure, filled with chairs and tables. A door at the far end stood open to the usual filthy kitchen, and a strong smell of urine hinted that the bathroom facilities were not far away. The television was on – a cricket match, of course – and about twenty men were watching it and drinking chai. They turned in surprise to look at me as I came in.

'Yes, Madame?' one man, whom I took to be the owner, asked.

'I was wondering if I could have a room for the night?'

He stared at me. 'Oh, Madame, there are no rooms here.'

The men weren't watching the cricket any more. They were openly staring at me. I got the feeling Rahimabad did not receive many overnight tourists.

'But the sign says "Hotel",' I said, pointing back outside. Even as I did, I experienced a sinking sensation, realizing that the sign was actually fiction, like so many others I had seen on my travels in Asia, such as those advertising hot showers; showers that turned out to be a bucket of tepid water.

'Restaurant, yes,' the same man said. 'We have roti, dahl.'

'You don't have any rooms?' I said again. In Rahimabad there was nowhere else to go; I had already seen all of it. 'Do you have any charpoys?'

He shook his head. We stared at each other. I stood there, rummaging in my head for ideas of what to do next. The daily bus to Karimabad had long since passed me on the road. There would be no others. It would soon be dark. I had a torch, but I did not want to walk in the dark to whatever next village lay down the road, where it was equally unlikely there would be a hotel. I thought uneasily of Muhammad and the way he had hissed, *There are bandits!*

'Madame!' The owner addressed me so loudly that I started. 'Madame, you can sleep here if you wish. When the restaurant closes. I will allow.'

So it was a hotel, after all. I was overcome with relief. 'Thank you!' I said. And then, 'Where do I sleep?'

'Down there,' he said, and waved a vague hand in the direction of the far end of the restaurant.

I didn't understand. 'There is a room outside?'

'No, no, no. This is not hotel!'

I was mystified. 'Where do I sleep?'

'I am telling you, sleeping *there*,' he said, waving his hand again towards the back wall of the restaurant. Where the chairs were stacked up.

'Oh,' I said. 'Now I see.'

His name was Arshad, and he was the only man there who spoke English. I was invited to sit and watch the cricket with them. I wished, not for the first time in Pakistan, that I knew something about the game. Arshad brought me dahl and rotis. As I ate, and my eyes became accustomed to the gloom of the dim light bulbs, I noticed a rifle propped behind his desk. When darkness fell around six, the men watching cricket drifted away in twos and threes. I stood by Arshad's desk and pointed to the rifle.

'What's that for?'

He took it up, and showed it to me. 'This one airgun. I use it for shooting birds.'

'Do you have a Kalashnikov?' I asked. 'I'd like to see one.'

Arshad looked at me with surprise. 'Not here, but at home I have a Kalashnikov.' Then he suddenly mimed putting a gun on his shoulder and firing, spraying the interior of the restaurant with imaginary bullets. 'Bam, bam, bam!'

I skipped to one side. 'Do you use it a lot?' I persisted. I thought it unlikely I would ever have the chance to have a conversation like this again.

'Once!' Arshad said loudly, still animated. 'Once, I had to use it. Twenty-five bullets in a round. All!' Then he looked at me. I have no idea what expression was on my face, but whatever it was, he stopped his Kalashnikov reverie as abruptly as he had begun it.

'Why?' I asked. 'When was that?'

'My English, it is not so good,' Arshad said, although we both knew by now that that was not true. He turned away, and went back to counting rupees.

When he had finished, and everything had been tidied, the generator for the television and the lights was unplugged outside.

'Back at 6 a.m., Madame,' Arshad said, giving me a candle before locking me in for the night. The door was bolted and padlocked from the outside.

At the far end of the room I arranged chairs against the wall in a row for a bed, like Snow White. I didn't want to dwell on the fact that I was locked in. It had happened before I realized what was going on. I wished I had the remainder of my bottle of bootleg Red Dragon Chinese whisky with me, but on that at least, I had taken Muhammad's advice. He had told me not to bring it with me, in case I was stopped and searched by the military and ended up having to pay a lot of baksheesh. I curled up and put my daypack under my head for a pillow. This was not how I had thought the day would end, and yet I was buzzing. I felt very, very alive.

As promised, Arshad returned at six the following morning, and I was back walking on the road very soon after. My destination that day was Nilt, where a Government Rest House awaited me. Among the books I had bought in Rawalpindi was E. F. Knight's 1895 *Where Three Empires Meet: A Narrative of Recent Travel in Kashmir, Western Tibet, Gilgit and the Adjoining Countries.*

One detail I had retained from Knight's book was the fact that when the British had fought the local people at the battle of Nilt in 1891, garnets were so plentiful that the local people used them as bullets. Knight writes of a wounded comrade who had been hit by one: 'This bullet, when extracted, was found to be a garnet enclosed in lead. There were sacks of similar bullets within the fort.'

I walked along the narrow valley road, with the vertical mountain walls leaning over me, and tried to imagine how hundreds of soldiers could have hidden in this landscape, where no cover seemed possible; garnet bullets punching through the air.

Rocks and rubble frequently tumbled down, in smaller and greater quantities, making me jumpy. For such a solid landscape, it seemed very fragile. I began to pass small white hand-painted signs that read 'Be Careful. You Are Entering Slide Area'. Further down the road, each one giving a different distance, signs would tell me to 'Relax. Slide Area Ends'. Sometimes the slide from the slide area had knocked the 'Be Careful' warning signs into the river valley below and I found myself being urged to Relax, without ever knowing I had been in the danger area. The whole place seemed like one gigantic 'Slide Area' to me.

Far above, packed snow lay in the gaps between mountains. As it melted, it would slowly slide further and further downwards until something gave and the whole lot roared down in an avalanche, taking any stones in its path and throwing them on to the road and into the river below.

I walked along quietly, listening hard for any sound of telltale dribbles of stones starting to fall. There was nowhere to go on the road, other than backwards or forwards. On my right side, the vertical mountain. On my left, a sheer drop to the Hunza River. I scurried along between the signs, breathing hard.

In the afternoon, I decided to hitch a lift. I had no definite idea of how far away Nilt was, and the prospect of relaxing at the Government Rest House after my night on the chairs was becoming more and more appealing. Besides, I had a longing to ride in a Bedford truck; I had been looking at them for days now.

The Bedford trucks that ply Pakistani roads are works of art; a travelling circus of marvellous, colourful kitsch. Inside the cab there are flashing fairy lights, tinsel trim around the windscreen, sparkly things, dangly things, quotations from the Koran, and a tiny, begrudging piece of clear windscreen in front of the driver. Outside, the panels of the trucks are painted with intricate mosaics of flowers, birds and trees, interspersed with ships and planes. The panels are framed in cut-out silver metal trims. Bits of mirrors are stuck on, with fringes of chains and coins hanging under the bumpers. They were fabulous.

The first truck I hitched stopped. 'Where you going?' the driver asked, looking down from the great height of his window.

'Nilt,' I said. I could see that the cab was already full: there were four men in there. I wasn't at all keen on the idea of sitting on someone's lap for the next hour or however long it would take to get to Nilt. I was not going to take this lift.

'OK up top?' the driver asked, indicating with his hand the metal ladder that led to a space above the cab.

I hadn't expected this. 'Sure!' I said, delightedly. I scrambled up the narrow ladder and jumped into the hollow structure that slanted far out over the cab. It was very high up, and when the truck started lumbering forward again I felt as if I was in a howdah, riding an uncertain elephant. The driver kept his hand constantly on the horn – the elephant trumpeting. Once, during the drive, I thought I heard a loud booming sound somewhere behind me, but I couldn't be sure, due to the constant noise of the horn. After being at ground level for the last two days, this sudden elevation into the landscape was stirring. My heart lurched in rhythm with the truck as we swayed along at speed, the wheels sometimes passing much closer than I liked to the sheer drop to the Hunza River. Thus, I arrived in Nilt, an hour or so later.

Nilt was located in a bend of the valley, with views out over Rakaposhi mountain. It was smaller than Rahimabad. There were two chai stalls, and a shack that sold nails, plastic flip-flops, tin plates and Chinese-made thermos flasks. I could not see anything that looked like a Government Rest House.

At one stall I drank chai and ate part of a rock-solid saffron-yellow cake, watching the game of invisible Ludo on a worn board being played on the road outside. I looked at the map again. There it was, 'GRH', Government Rest House. Except it wasn't. The map was all hearsay and rumour. A man appeared beside me and introduced himself. Hameed was an engineer. I was to discover that even the smallest Pakistani mountain villages had an engineer's office. It was a full-time job to valiantly try and control the roads and bridges that were imposed on this mobile, ever-shifting landscape.

I showed him the map, with the rest house clearly marked. He shrugged his shoulders. 'Once, yes. Not now. Now there is no place to stay.'

'What happened to it?' I asked. 'The rest house?' I had no idea where I was going to stay that night, but it suddenly seemed futile to worry about it. Everything would work out, somehow.

Hameed looked sheepish. 'It was there,' he said eventually, pointing to the building just behind us. 'But now it is office. My office.'

Hameed's office had a concrete floor, maps of the surrounding mountain valleys and roads on the wall, and only one chair. But it had a big square wooden table.

'You can stay the night here,' he said, giving me the key. Later, he sent his young son up with a bowl of dahl and rotis. I ate it gratefully, sitting on the step that overlooked the street, as the sun went down. I had made it this far.

That night, I locked myself in Hameed's office, stretched out on his table, and slept.

When I walked into the Hunza Lodge in Karimabad the following day, my arrival caused a stir.

'How you get here?' the owner Iqbal said, staring at me uneasily. 'No Gilgit bus today!' He called his friends in from the chai stall across the street. They stood and stared at me. I stared back, wondering what was going on. On that third morning out of Gilgit, I had abandoned my attempt to walk to Karimabad. The only portable food I could find in the chai stalls of Nilt were dried apricots and more of that hard yellow cake, which I did not think was enough to fuel a day's walk. And sleeping on a row of chairs one night and a table the next, however novel, had not been exactly restful. So I had hitched the rest of the way to Karimabad, in a jeep this time, arriving around noon.

'No Gilgit bus coming today,' another of them said. He looked spooked.

'I didn't come from Gilgit,' I said. 'I came from Nilt this morning. By jeep.'

'Gilgit road is blocked since yesterday. Avalanche. No buses coming,' Iqbal said.

I discovered that between Rahimabad and Nilt, on the stretch of road I had walked and hitched the previous day, a huge landslide caused by an avalanche higher up now blocked the road. Teams on both sides of the landslide were working on clearing it, but today no vehicles in either direction would get through, and probably none tomorrow either. I thought of the little white hand-painted signs I had walked past. 'Be Careful. You Are Now Entering Slide Area'.

'You are lucky!' Iqbal said, when I explained how I had travelled from Gilgit.

Rattled, I retreated to my room. It had an actual bed, and I lay down for a while, trying not to wonder which part of the road had been blocked, and how long after I had walked past the place the landslide had come rushing down. I wondered if that had been the booming sound I thought I had heard while in the howdah of the Bedford the previous afternoon. It was better, I decided, not to dwell on it.

Karimabad, a tiny village built into the slope of a mountain, had extraordinary views over Rakaposhi and valleys of flowering apricot trees. As it was off-season, none of the big brand-new ugly hotels on the edge of town had yet opened; these had been built to accommodate the people who came and went to China on tour buses. There were also several other guesthouses of the type I was staying in.

In Karimabad, I became temporarily obsessed with food. I sat on the balcony in front of my room that first afternoon, looking out over one of the most astonishing views I've ever seen, and all I could think about was food. Breakfast since arrival in Pakistan had mostly been paratha, a kind of deep-fried roti that came in a plateful of oil. If I was lucky, lunch was aloo, curried potato and eggs. If not, dahl and rotis, which was also dinner, unless I wanted goat curry, which I never did. Having seen the state of too many filthy kitchens, I was sticking with vegetarian food in northern Pakistan. I liked dahl and rotis, which was lucky, but my Western palate was also craving some variety. I went on a hunt.

Along with a couple of antique shops on the main street, there was a tiny trekking shop in Karimabad. Northern Pakistan has five of the fourteen highest mountains in the world; all starting above 8,000 metres. Most are in the Karakorams, including the second-highest mountain in the world, K2; infamous for being far more difficult to ascend than Everest. There are many mountaineering expeditions, and every year at the end of the season, the expeditions get rid of some of their supplies and kit. Or at least, they did when I was there: the tiny trekking shop behind the Hunza Lodge contained evidence of this practice.

It was full of battered tents, second-hand crampons, cooking stoves, half-full canisters of camping gas and smelly sleeping bags. I wasn't interested in any of those. What I was interested in were the leftover food supplies, clearly the dregs of what had once been there. There were half-full packets of Cup-a-Soup, out-of-date tins of Spam, powdered milk, handfuls of broken spaghetti, and packets of freeze-dried potato. I hunted through the shelves, where everything was shoved together, hoping for something better than tins of out-of-date Spam.

The owner tried to interest me in more lucrative items of merchandise. 'You want tent, Madame?' he asked, holding up one of the less thrashed-looking tents.

'No thanks.'

'Maybe rucksack? I have good one. Berghaus.'

'I already have a rucksack.'

'You want stove?'

'No thanks.'

He kept trying. 'Sleeping bag? Ice axe?' He held up each of these items in turn, before dropping them back on the floor.

'No thanks.'

'What you want, Madame?'

'These,' I said joyously, turning from the leftover food shelves, two tins in my hands. I had found one tin of Australian Cheddar and one tin of Indonesian tuna. I had had no idea Cheddar cheese could come in a tin, and I have never seen one since. Their labels were half torn off and both tins were significantly dented, but they were in date, and that was good enough for me.

I sat out on the balcony of the Hunza Lodge that afternoon, having spent some happy minutes meditating on which tin I would open first, devouring hunks of cheese with rotis. I was finishing off some letters. I was always writing letters back then, and most of them were to Jake, the eternal ghost beside me on that journey. *I will stand still for you, while you explore the world*, he had written. *I don't want you to stand still*, I thought, when I read that. *I want us both to explore the world together*. From time to time, I heard noises, loud as explosions. After the third one, I went in search of Iqbal.

'What are those noises?'

'Glaciers cracking.'

I went back to my letter to Jake. I wrote: *I am listening to glaciers cracking.*

On that journey, the first thing I did in every new place I arrived was locate the nearest post office. The one in Karimabad was tiny. I arrived there with a handful of letters, in search of the pot of glue every post office in Pakistan had. The locally bought envelopes were not gummed, and you had to glue them shut in the post office. I glued the envelopes of my letters to Jake and to family and friends back in Ireland, and waited to hear the postage rates.

Jake's was easy. 'England, yes?'

'Actually, Scotland, but part of Britain, yes.' A number of stamps were duly glued to Jake's letter; the stamps didn't have gum either.

'These ones?' The man in the post office peered uncertainly at my Irish-addressed envelopes. 'What country is this?'

'Ireland,' I said.

'Ah, Holland!' he replied.

This was common. Whenever I said 'Ireland', someone invariably reparteed with 'Holland'. I had discovered that this was because, unlike Ireland, Holland, which sounded only a tiny bit like Ireland, had a cricket team, and the international language of Pakistan was cricket.

'No, not Holland. Ireland. Eye-err-land.' I wrote it down. The post office official had never heard of Ireland.

He continued to hunt through his copy of the *Pakistani Postal Workers' Handbook*, while I waited. 'Madame, I cannot find this country,' he said eventually. He flapped the pages of

the book at me. 'Is not on my list, therefore cannot be sending letters there!'

It's a bizarre experience to be told by someone in a post office far from home that your country does not officially exist. He passed the handbook over to me, and I searched, myself. I looked for Ireland; Republic of Ireland; and even Eire, but none of those names were there. He was right. Ireland was nowhere to be found. 'It's not there,' I said in disbelief.

'You see!' the post office official said triumphantly. 'This Ireland is not on my list!' He pushed the Irish-addressed letters back across the counter to me, still minus their stamps.

'But I want to send them,' I persisted, pushing them back to him. 'I know they'll get there. Honestly, there really is an Ireland.' It was one of the most surreal conversations of my life.

'Perhaps,' the official then said, 'you could send instead these letters to Holland. I am knowing the rates for Holland.' What he meant was, he would send the letters to Ireland for Holland rates.

And so, my letters to Ireland, a country that didn't officially exist in 1995 in the mountains of northern Pakistan, were finally posted.

After a few days spent exploring Karimabad, Baltit and Gulmit, I took the nice bus back to Gilgit. Through some grapevine process, Muhammad had known I'd made it safely to Karimabad. He was still a bit mad at me.

'Crazy! You crazy, Rosita!' He scolded me, while getting my rucksack out of the cupboard where it had been stored in my absence. My former room was still empty. He carried my rucksack across the garden. 'Where you go next?' He looked back at me warily, wondering what new unsuitable plan I was scheming.

'Skardu,' I said. 'Don't worry, Muhammad, I'm going to take the bus there.'

Skardu, the capital of Baltistan, is 170 kilometres southeast of Gilgit. I was still enthralled by the vertical landscape of the Karakoram, and wanted to spend more time among the mountains. Expeditions started out to K2 from Skardu. I had a vague idea in my head of absorbing some sense of the possibilities of adventure just by being there.

My guidebook told of incredible scenery, and villages untouched by modernity. An air route to Islamabad had only been established in the 1960s. The road I was about to travel, the Indus Highway, was completed in 1985. The knowledge that it was only a decade since Baltistan had had a road to connect it with the wider world was somehow intoxicating. This was not a world I knew anything about.

Two days later, I was aboard the local bus from Gilgit to Skardu. I had said goodbye to Muhammad a second time, telling him I'd be back in a week or ten days. This time, though, I took my rucksack.

The guidebook instructed, 'For the best views, sit on the right side of the bus heading to Skardu.' I had duly found a window seat on the right-hand side. Women in Pakistani buses that are not minibuses are seated together, but I was the only woman on the entire bus, which was, of course, full. The driver formally asked if I would share my double seat with a man in a cream shalwar kameez, who hovered apologetically in the aisle.

'Madame, you maybe permit me to sit?' he said, bowing.

'Of course.'

He sat in beside me and at once fell asleep. About an hour after we had left Gilgit behind, the landscape began to change dramatically. We had crossed a suspension bridge over the Indus River, and were now on the Indus Highway proper. The road takes its name from the river, which it shadows almost the entire way to Skardu. The Indus, which is 2,880 kilometres long, starts in Tibet, carves its way through Ladakh in northern India, along the valleys and gorges that divide the Himalayas and the Karakoram range that we were now travelling through, south to the Punjab and Sind, until it enters the Arabian Sea just east of Karachi.

One thing I had learned in northern Pakistan was that the word 'Highway' bore no relation to what I knew as highways. The further we travelled along the grandly named Indus Highway, the less it even resembled a road, far less a broad and surfaced piece of infrastructure. We were on an unsurfaced track, which had no protective barriers, and the track was now following the Indus River. Not alongside it, but far, far above: hundreds of metres above the gorge.

Slowly the road began to take on the sensation of fiction. It was literally carved out of the side of a mountain gorge. From where I sat, in my unluckily scenic right-hand seat, the bus appeared to be levitating in thin air, so narrow was the road, and so close were the wheels to its bare edge. Far above us on the left, the gorge walls extended upwards hundreds of metres to a strip of sky as defined and narrow as a runway. Far, far down below, the Indus glittered like polished steel. It took its colour from the glacier waters that fed it; a shade of grey-green I had never seen before. The Indus was half a mile wide, but from where our bus crawled along, it looked no wider than a goat track.

We started to hit the hairpin bends, the bus labouring and the brakes screeching as we rounded each dreadful turn. I stared transfixed out the window. I did not want to believe my eyes. The landscape was almost savage in its nightmarish beauty. I was barely able to comprehend its vast, surreal scale. Outlandish, I thought. Not of this world.

Before this journey, my fears of travelling on a local bus in Asia had been of ending up under a rockfall, or of the over-loaded bus toppling over, or of our bus crashing in the dark because the headlights weren't on and some truck had run into us. On this particular bus journey, I realized I had wasted so much energy in the past worrying about the bad things that might happen. They were just possibilities. Whereas this – this ghastly, unprotected vertical drop to the Indus far below – was a reality, just mere inches from the edges of tyres I knew would be bald.

The man beside me snored gently. I envied him with every cell of my body. I don't know how long I sat like that, rigid by the window. Suddenly I became aware that the road was widening, the arid landscape opening out into green, like a concertina being pulled slightly, and we were stopping. Had we arrived in Skardu?

We had not arrived in Skardu. We were in the tiny vil-lage of Thowar. The land had levelled out into a kind of shelf under the mountain, where a few hundred souls had chosen to perch themselves, like birds on the highest swaying branch of a tree. The village, no bigger than a small field, was irrigated, and the green glow was a shock after hours of grey rock and stone. Snug, stone-built houses and apricot trees were planted right up to that vertical drop. We had stopped to offload var-ious sacks of produce from the roof. The driver handed a

bundle of letters out through the window. The children clus-
tered around the bus. They caught sight of me, and jumped up
and down, windmilling their arms in wide-eyed amazement.

There was a second tiny village, further along the track:
Basho. It too was a small irrigated space, the village bordered
on one side by the drop to the gorge, and on the other, by
the mountain face. They were so small, we left each of them
behind in less than half a minute. I turned round in my seat as
we left Basho and saw the green created by the irrigation line
vanish almost immediately. Among the dark shadows cast by
the mountain walls, and the black of the stone, the villages of
Thowar and Basho glowed with the luminosity of tiny chips of
emeralds.

From their location in the gorge, I realized, the people
in those villages would never see either sunrise or sunset.
The sky was a strip between the walls of the gorge high above.
The only time sunlight would hit the villages was when the
sun was directly overhead. I thought of the children who had
gestured to me. What was it like to live in a landscape that was
vertical, and where there were no horizons? I imagined them
growing up fearless of vertigo, playing their games on those
tightropes of land, dreaming of some day seeing the sky in its
entirety. It kept my mind off the road for at least five minutes.

The only other signs of human settlement along the way
were occasional roofless cottages and pitiful makeshift tents,
clinging like stoic barnacles to the mountain side of the track.
They provided shelter for the men whose Sisyphean task it
was to attempt to keep the Indus Highway clear of the debris
from landslides and rockfalls. We passed small groups of men
labouring with shovels and pickaxes, a wheelbarrow by their
side. The rocks in the wheelbarrow were tipped into the maw

of the gorge, far, far below. I could not imagine a worse job than this Russian roulette joust with nature.

The man beside me had finally woken up. We had just come upon a fresh rockfall that had spread right across the track, making it impossible to pass. A party of men was working on it. The bus stopped. We sat there for a long time, waiting.

The driver sounded his horn. I could not think why. It was obvious we were waiting for the track to be cleared.

'Not good,' the man beside me said, twisting into the aisle to look.

'Why?' I said immediately, my heart beginning to beat faster.

'We cannot wait here long,' he explained. 'We are still four hours from Skardu. The driver has to get to Skardu before dark. He cannot drive this road in the dark.'

The thought of continuing this horrific journey in darkness made my hands go clammy. 'Perhaps we could all get out and help move the rocks?' I managed, but realized as I did that the bus was moving again. The driver drove the bus almost up to the rockfall. Then he got out and conferred with the men, indicating a small gap they had opened up between the rockfall and the very edge of the track. In rising terror, I saw that he intended to try and get the bus through this space, which looked no wider than a wheelbarrow.

The driver got on again, and revved up. Everyone fell silent. I had never been on an Asian bus before where everyone suddenly stopped talking; in itself, a deeply unsettling sign. It was not just my palms that were clammy, but my spine, all the way up to my neck. The bus jerked forward. The driver drove on to the pile of rocks on the left side of the cleared space; the gorge lay below on the right. The bus was now tilted at an angle of about 35 degrees towards the gorge, and, apart from the supplies that had been offloaded at Thowar and Basho, many sacks of cargo remained tied to the roof. We edged forward. The bus groaned, struggling with gravity.

In those moments, I truly believed death was imminent. I was paralysed with terror; fearing the wheels' loss of purchase, and the freefall of the bus into the gorge below. I was utterly overtaken by a sensation of horror and impending disaster. I thought I was going to black out. I closed my eyes. I couldn't look out the window any longer. In those moments, when I believed we were all at risk of dying, scenes from my life did not flash before me. I did not see Jake's face, or anyone's face: the image that came into my head was the wholly banal one of the unfinished cup of coffee I had left behind at the Madina earlier that day, because I was running late; an image that seemed to me now had come from another, different world that had existed before I had got on the bus.

Then all four wheels of the bus thumped down together.

There followed another four hours of this terrible journey. Near Kachura, the landscape finally opened up and the road drifted ever downwards to the bottom of the river valley. We were past the gorges. I lay against the window, stunned at simply still being alive. I had spent the last four hours with only one thought in my head: how was I going to get out of Baltistan again? The Indus Highway was the only road in and thus the only road out. I had no idea how I would do it, but I vowed to myself over and over that it would not be by way of the local bus on the Indus Highway.

A couple of kilometres out of Skardu there was an army checkpoint. The bus stopped, and two soldiers with guns got on, walking up and down, asking random passengers questions. I stared out the window. Alongside the checkpoint was a large square building. Painted on the gable wall in large faded white letters, five words in English spelt a surreal, arcane greeting to Baltistan. They read: *Welcome To The World Without.*

Skardu's defining feature is the colossal rock that lies to the west of the town, in the centre of a steep-sided river valley. It reminded me of the shape of an upturned ark, hull to the sky and who knew what cargo hidden deep within the arid ground. The town crouched at the eastern side of the rock, in the centre of a plain 13 kilometres wide and 32 kilometres long. Every afternoon, there were dust storms, carried down the mountains from Ladakh and beyond; small pieces of grit that got into everything, from my eyes to the pages of my diary. There was once a lake in this river valley; water where Skardu's bazaar and narrow side streets now stood. I was to wake one night in Skardu, having dreamed I was drowning; that there was water up to my pillow, that the rock had righted itself and was now floating, and that the whole town was adrift, unfastened from its uneasy moorings of concrete.

I was staying at the Baltistan Tourist Cottage, halfway down Naya Bazaar. It was not a cottage, and nor were there any tourists there, apart from me. It fronted the noisy bazaar; a concrete box over a shop, with a corrugated iron roof. My spartan room, Number 4, was at the back and overlooked the ark. It didn't have electricity, even when it wasn't a load-shedding night. I had the luxury of an attached tiny concrete bathroom with a squat toilet, and a tap with cold water on the wall. A bucket of tepid water was left outside my door each morning.

When I had signed the register on arrival, I checked it to see if any other tourists had stayed recently. They had not. The trekking season had not yet begun. Iqbal, the owner, craned his neck to see where I had travelled from that day.

'Gilgit,' he said. 'First bus from Gilgit in five days. Road was blocked until today.'

'Iqbal,' I asked hesitantly, not at all sure I wanted to know the answer to my question, 'are there many accidents on the Indus Highway?'

'Many, many accidents!' he said. 'The army drivers, always they are in too much hurry; not going slow around corners. Always their jeeps are falling off the road!'

'And the buses?' I asked weakly. 'What about the buses?'

'Buses too.'

'Recently?'

'Yes, yes, recently. One year ago was last time.'

'Into the river? All lost?' I could not believe I had started this conversation. I held on to the edge of his desk and saw again the Indus far below me, the mountains far above me, and the eroded edge of the track beside me. I saw so clearly the bus falling; a waterfall of metal and glass, of flapping shalwars and roped-in baggage, of screams and rushing air, and then uneasy ripples contracting slowly on the grey-green surface of the Indus.

'Inshallah. All,' he admitted, and shrugged his shoulders. 'Tourists also. Gone for ever,' he added.

The very first thing I did in Skardu was to visit the Pakistan International Airlines (PIA) office, which was just a room under the Sadpara Hotel on Yadgar Chowk. It was sad, but I would not be seeing Muhammad and the Madina Hotel ever again; I was not going back to Gilgit on that unspeakable road. I would fly out of Skardu to Islamabad instead.

I marched purposefully into the tiny office. I had done my research. The planes were always over-booked, but two seats were reserved on every flight for tourists. One of them was going to be mine, a week hence.

'Madame?' the clerk asked.

'I want to buy a ticket to Islamabad,' I said confidently. 'For one week's time.' As all my travel on this journey had so far been done on local buses and trains, I had no idea how much an internal flight in Pakistan would be. I didn't care. If it cost all the money I had left on my American Express traveller's cheques, I was going to hand the lot over to the clerk.

He looked at me. 'Sit down, please,' he said. 'First you are needing to know more about this flight.'

Over green tea, he explained clearly and patiently to me the unique set of circumstances that determined whether or not the morning plane from Islamabad would arrive in Skardu. Due to the fact that the whole area we were in was composed of mountains and glaciers, it made take-off and landing totally weather-dependent. He didn't add difficult. He let me figure that out for myself. The closest most planes go near mountains is flying high above them. In Baltistan, to get into Skardu, the plane needed to descend from cruising altitude while flying through – or, more accurately, between – the mountains. To depart, it had to fly through and between the mountains again before reaching cruising altitude. For this fantastical aeronautical achievement, the pilot needed total visibility, for reasons so obvious even I could figure them out.

'Therefore the plane can only be landing in good weather. If there is cloud, there is no flight. Sometimes, the plane takes off from Islamabad and has to turn back if cloud is coming. We need a two-hour visibility window, because the plane needs to go back again to Islamabad. PIA cannot be having a 737 grounded in Skardu. Last year, plane had to stay here one week. Very big loss to the company.'

'Did the plane go today?' I asked, suddenly acutely aware of the weather. It was cloudy and dull outside, and had rained in the night.

'No plane today. Clouds.' He indicated the phone on his desk. 'Every morning, we wait for Islamabad to call at 9.40 a.m. to see if plane is coming.' He indicated the many chairs in the room; I had vaguely noticed there seemed to be a lot of chairs in a very small office. 'Passengers must come here every morning and wait for the phone call, or send a runner. The decision to fly is only made at the last moment; when everyone is seated. Once the plane leaves Islamabad, it will be here in forty-five minutes, and it needs to depart again immediately.'

'So what happens to those passengers today?' I asked. 'Do they fly tomorrow? If there is a plane?'

'No,' the clerk said. 'Today's passengers will not be flying tomorrow, because there was no flight yesterday either. It was the passengers from yesterday who were due to fly today. Everyone has to wait when there is no plane coming. You could buy a ticket today for next week, but plane might not be coming.'

I could see how the whole schedule was always tumbling like dominoes. Buying a plane ticket was basically a lottery with the weather. There was nothing I could do about that.

But I would not be constantly shoved to the back of the waiting list, because of the fact that two seats every day were allocated to tourists. I would be fine. 'There are always two seats kept for tourists, so I will be able to get out, yes?'

'Maybe not,' was the unwelcome answer. 'At the moment, there are no tourists, so we sell those two seats every day to other people. They will be before you if plane is cancelled before you fly.'

I digested this.

'Madame, there is a bus, going to Gilgit every day. From there you can get a bus to Islamabad. The plane is sometimes very difficult.'

'I am not going on the bus,' I said stoutly. 'How much is the ticket to Islamabad?' And now my precious ticket was folded into the money belt under my clothes, where I kept my passport and traveller's cheques.

The bazaar at Skardu held none of the follies of Gilgit's bazaar with its bunches of artificial flowers, bales of fabric and stacks of luridly coloured tea sets. Instead, it traded in lumps of medieval-smelling smoked cheese, chunks of pink rock salt, and candles that fizzled like sparklers when I lit them. One stall sold jars of something called Invisible Face Cream. Suzukis and jeeps tore up and down, streaked with the dust that got into everything. As I walked around the morning after arriving in Skardu, I became aware that there was something strange about the place.

It took me a while to realize that there were no women visible anywhere. Unlike the other parts of Pakistan I had travelled in, Skardu was Shia Muslim, and their women appeared to live in purdah. The entire time I spent in Skardu, I did not see a single woman in public. I also realized that, if I thought it was strange to be in a place where others of my gender were completely invisible, I was myself an object of immense strangeness to the local people.

I soon discovered that I was the sole tourist in Skardu. Even though I was always covered, dressed in the shalwar kameez I had bought in Delhi's Parj Ganj market, it didn't seem to make much difference. I also had a dupatta, a head-scarf, which I hadn't bothered with much elsewhere in Pakistan, but in Skardu I wore it all the time, even indoors, at the Tourist Cottage.

To my dismay, I found that every time I went out I immediately attracted enormous attention. I did not have to guess what people were thinking. Men stared at me openly, with vivid expressions ranging from amazement to contempt. Lines of small boys followed me everywhere, as if I was some unwilling Pied Piper. When I stopped to look back at them, they stopped too and regarded me with solemnity. When I continued, they continued. I wrapped my dupatta closely around my face, so there was not much of it visible, but nothing could mask the fact of my presence. Just by being there, I was strange and different.

Like every road I travelled in Baltistan, the road to Shigar was terrible. It took me days in Skardu to get up the courage to make another journey by road. I had fallen into a torpor, sitting on the balcony of the Tourist Cottage, drinking the green tea Ali, the kitchen boy, brought me and staring down at the bazaar below. I felt somehow paralysed there, unable to contemplate either travelling further away from Skardu, further into the valleys and glaciers, or leaving it altogether. At night, I could not sleep. I watched the moon rise over the ark of Skardu Rock. I lit candles and wrote to Jake, although how my letters were ever to make it out of this place I did not know. In those long nights, it seemed impossible that I would ever see him again, or indeed anyone else I knew. That world was so unfamiliar to this place that it felt to me like somewhere from science fiction. I finally slept and dreamed again of falling to the bottom of the green-grey Indus.

Eventually, one day, I gave Iqbal my rucksack to store in a cupboard, and allowed Ali to escort me to a cargo jeep departing at noon from the far end of the bazaar. I had to do something; go somewhere to escape from my bad dreams and the bazaar full of staring eyes.

I firmly commandeered the passenger side, on the left, thinking that I would be away from any more possible precipices.

Half an hour into the journey to Shigar, I realized I had chosen to sit on the wrong side of the jeep. My left-hand position gave me a full, uninterrupted view of the gorge we were travelling above. The jeep felt heavy and clumsy and too big for the narrow track. The gorge below was nothing compared to the Indus Gorge, but I still sat there rigidly, willing the journey to end very soon and wondering if, in Pakistan, I had become a person who was always going to be afraid of things.

Shigar was like a place from a fairy tale. It had the most idyllic and beautiful setting, at the mouth of a vast alluvial valley that unfolded endlessly behind it. It looked ancient, with its stone buildings and their intricately hand-carved wooden lintels and window frames. The houses were low, flat-roofed, made of cut stone. A yak's head was nailed above every door. There was a wooden mosque, with carved windows of latticework. Its open door had several different kinds of carving around the frame, and as we passed by I could see a corbelled wooden roof and carpets glowing on the floor within. The narrow lanes were white with fallen apricot blossoms, from the orchards that were everywhere. A small river ran through the village, delicate bridges arching over it at intervals.

The children gathered as soon as I stepped out of the jeep. I was staying that night in the Government Rest House, an edifice that definitely existed this time, unlike the one I had tried to stay at in Nilt. I had the chit to prove it.

The driver of the jeep said something to the children, and then turned to me. 'They will bring you to the rest house.'

I was led by dancing and skipping children through the scented lanes of Shigar and the calm riverside to the edge of the village, where the Government Rest House stood. When we reached the gate, they fled, ducked around the backs of houses and stuck their heads out, waiting to see what I would do next.

Every rest house has a chowkidar, a word I loved. This is a caretaker, who lives nearby and who holds the keys to the rest house. On hearing the commotion of the children, a very, very old man appeared from the house opposite and slowly came to meet me at the gate. He examined my chit, then produced an enormous key that again looked like something from a fairy tale, as if it would open a castle.

The rest house was the most opulent building I had seen in many weeks. My room had dark red carpet, two beds, an armchair and a coffee table – an item of furniture I hadn't seen since leaving England. There was a vast bathroom whose white walls were tiled, not grey unplastered concrete, like every other bathroom I had used in northern Pakistan. There was a large white china washbasin that looked Victorian, and probably was. There was a white china elephant's feet squat toilet. There was an actual showerhead, which I eyed with excitement: I had become used to washing in a bucket of water. However, there were limits to my new luxury. When I put my hand under the showerhead in delighted expectation, there was no hot water in the shower; in fact there was no running water in the bathroom at all. Nor was there electricity.

That afternoon, I set out to hike the small stony hill that overlooks Shigar. Up there somewhere on the rough trail were ancient Buddhist stupas and stone carvings that I had heard about in Skardu. It was hot and cloudless. I walked along the village's irrigation channels, then picked my way carefully up the steep scree slope. For half an hour or so, I climbed steadily upwards. Then I heard noises behind me, and looked back down the hill.

Some of the children who had accompanied me from the jeep to the rest house were following me up the hill. They were much faster than me. In less than ten minutes, they were no more than 20 metres from me; then they stopped. They jumped up and down, shouting. Thinking they would go away soon, I ignored them and carried on up the hill. They continued to follow, always keeping the same distance.

After a while, I sat down to rest. The children stopped too. I counted them. There were eleven: eight boys, three girls, one carrying a tiny baby. They were not all young children; some of the boys looked like teenagers. They shrieked with delight when I sat down and looked at them. They pushed each other, and scuffled steadily closer to me. The baby cried.

I did not see the first stone. I heard a kind of movement in the air, then registered a sharp pain in my right arm. Another stone quickly followed, and then another and yet another. On the scree slope, there was a plentiful store of ammunition. The children's aim was good: all the stones found their target. They hurt. It took me some moments to register that I was being stoned. By then, all the children had stones in their hands, even the small girl with the crying baby on her hip. The stones were hitting my torso, and my arms. One the size of a fist just missed my face; I saw it go by in my peripheral vision.

The stone that had missed my head shocked me into action. I sprang to my feet and started yelling. 'Stop! Stop! Stop throwing those fucking stones! Go away!'

The children howled with laughter and fled down the hill. I watched them go, suddenly feeling shaky, and sat down again. I had thought how charming it was to be guided to the rest house by the skipping, laughing children of the village. What had made them change? Why had they stoned me on the hill, but not on the way to the rest house? At what point in their journey from the village had their behaviour begun to change? Was it beyond the irrigation channel? Halfway up the hill? When they were out of sight of the village? Did they always stone tourists, or just those tourists who were women on their own?

That evening, the chowkidar came with curried potatoes, chapattis, green tea, and a paraffin lamp. He lit the lamp, showed me how to turn it off, and left. The daylight was almost gone; I went out on to the veranda to watch the last of it fade. Clouds were creeping down the mountains like a diaphanous snow line, and a mist from the valley was rising slowly up to meet them.

People I had met on this journey, and others, were always telling me how brave I was to be travelling alone. I have never felt brave. Local people, of course, as in Pakistan, just thought I was crazy, not brave. The fact is, I wasn't brave at all. You are only brave when you do something you are afraid of, and although lots of times I did not like it at all, as now, I wasn't afraid of travelling alone. There were things I was deeply afraid of along the way, such as the thought of travelling on the local bus back to Gilgit, but I would not allow myself to be afraid of travelling alone. What was the alternative? Deny myself all these experiences on the road, the marvellous as well as the difficult ones? Stay at home and never go anywhere? It's that thought, the one of involuntary stasis, that has always filled me with genuine fear.

The pay-off for the travelling I love so much to do and the elsewhere I love to be in is the intermittent deep loneliness that is sometimes overwhelming. There is always a time in every journey I make when I fall into a lake of loneliness. In Pakistan I was often lonely, but Shigar that night was where I was loneliest of all. That night in Shigar, out on the veranda as the landscape slowly disappeared under cloud and mist, I had never felt more alone, or lonelier. Why had I chosen to come here? What was I doing here, in a place where men looked at you with contempt on the street and children stoned you? Why was this journey turning out to be so hard and so strange? Why had I not thrown away the piece of white card-board I had found at the bottom of my bag all those weeks later after the funeral in Edinburgh?

I had no answers for myself. The lamp glowed pale yellow on the veranda, like a small trapped moon. I was grateful for its light, even though I knew I would have to turn it off before I went to bed and watch the darkness settle in the room around me.

When I got back to Skardu, Iqbal told me there had been no plane that morning. I was due to fly out the next day.

'This April bad one. Many flights cancelled! Last April, every day going.'

I took my rucksack from the cupboard and Iqbal gave me back the key to Room 4. I was beginning to hate this room. There had been a problem with the water the day before, and it was worse now. There was no water in the cold tap, and the drains of the building had backed up. The smell was permeating everything. I was still the only guest in the Tourist Cottage, and the only tourist in town.

That afternoon, I returned to the PIA office.

'Flight today did not go, Madame,' the clerk told me. 'Forecast for tomorrow is not good. Much raining and clouds coming.'

'So what happens with my booking for tomorrow?' I asked.

The clerk shrugged. 'Tomorrow, if there is a plane, you cannot fly. You must wait till backlog clears. Two more days, maybe three, maybe more if no plane coming tomorrow either.'

Although I had not made any plans on this journey, other than making my way ever westwards overland, I had one deadline I needed to keep. My Iranian visa started running in less than ten days, which was why I was becoming so anxious about finding a way to leave Baltistan.

I had planned on taking the Quetta Express from Rawalpindi, a 32-hour journey across 1,200 kilometres, and then, from Quetta, making my way to the border town of Taftan and across into Zahedan in Iran from there. I had it all roughly figured out. I had my chador in my rucksack and I had my visa. But first, I had to get out of Baltistan. By plane, not bus.

From the PIA office, I went to a local trekking office. I had been in Asia long enough by then to know that strings could be pulled in almost any situation, whether aided by baksheesh or not. If there were meant to be two seats reserved each day for tourists, I was determined that I was going to get one of them, already sold to someone else or not.

'Can you help?' I asked the owner, Iskander, bluntly. 'I need to get on that plane tomorrow.'

Iskander picked up the phone and made some calls. It took a long time, and involved considerable shouting. Eventually, he clapped the phone down. 'It is done!' he announced triumphantly. 'Tomorrow morning, at 9.30 a.m., you must go with your luggage to the PIA office and wait to hear from Islamabad. They will have a seat for you. But of course,' he added, frowning, 'it is never certain if the plane can come or not.'

Ali was awaiting me, hanging over the balcony as usual. He called to me when I ascended the concrete stairway, pulling out the usual chair and table to set up for me on the balcony. He told me he was making green tea, and then vanished to bring the daily bucket of water. I did not want any more green tea, and I was sick of washing in barely tepid water. I was sick of being stared at. I was sick of being the only woman visible in Skardu. I was sick of testing myself and pushing myself so hard to see what I could endure. I was sick of being in love with a man on the other side of the world; a man who was wrecking my head by saying he was waiting for me to come back, and yet still remained in his former relationship.

I was in a foul humour. I did not go on to the balcony and drink kind Ali's green tea. I lay on my bed and raged; at my own cowardice for not being able to face the bus a second time, at the fact that it was weeks since I had been able to pick up any letters from Jake, at the fact that I was even writing to Jake. When I had stopped raging, I felt utterly desolate.

There was a huge thunderstorm that night in Skardu. I watched it from my bedroom window. Eerie streaks of lightning lit up the upturned ark of Skardu Rock. The river began to rise. The rain fell for hours. It was landslide weather.

In the morning, I had no appetite for breakfast. The dining-room roof was leaking copiously. Ali ran to and fro, placing bowls and saucepans under the many drips. Clouds had buried the mountains.

'Is not looking good for plane coming,' Iqbal said portentously, when I went to pay and go through what we all already knew was the charade of checking out. The plane was not going to fly in this weather.

'Goodbye, Iqbal. Goodbye, Ali,' I said. They just smiled at me.

I walked down the street with my rucksack to the PIA office. It was 9.30 a.m. and the office was already full. There were lines of jeeps and Suzukis and taxis waiting outside to transport people to the airport if the plane was coming.

At 9.40, punctually, the clerk's phone rang. It was a short call. 'Plane is cancelled,' he announced. A sigh went around the room. He started re-stamping tickets. People drifted away, as did all the vehicles around the PIA building.

Ali was watching for me from the balcony, green tea brewing, my chair pulled out. Iqbal was waiting with the register. I signed in again. In Room 4 I unpacked again and stared once more at the huge rock of Skardu. It was only then that I began to feel true panic and claustrophobia. For how many days was I going to have to go through the pantomime of packing and unpacking my rucksack, of checking in and checking out? I thought of the lines in 'Hotel California': 'You can check out any time you like, but you can never leave.' Another day lost in the attempt to get to the Iranian border before my visa expired. The Indus Highway lay like purgatory between my past and my future. I was never, ever going to get out of Baltistan, trapped there in paralysis by my own fears and the uncontrollable weather.

The next morning was exactly the same.

On the morning of the third day, clouds sliced the mountains in neat halves. Visibility looked poor. The plane was definitely not coming today. I packed my rucksack. I checked out. 'Goodbye, Iqbal. Goodbye, Ali.'

In the PIA office, 9.40 a.m. came and went without the phone ringing. I was standing in the doorway staring up at the clouds, wondering if I would have enough money and enough nerve to hire a jeep and driver to drive me, very, very slowly, to Gilgit, when people suddenly began to rush past me.

'Plane is coming!' the cry went up. People were flinging their bags into jeeps and taxis and taking off for the airport. Disbelievingly, I looked at the clerk. 'The plane has left Islamabad!' he shouted at me. 'You must go at once to the airport!'

The next minutes were a complete blur. I found a taxi and jumped in. 'Plane is coming!' the taxi driver said. The taxi hurtled down Skardu's Naya Bazaar. I twisted to look back at the place I had not fully believed I would ever leave and knew I would never see again.

The plane was just landing on the runway when we arrived. I have never seen such chaos in an airport before or since. The tiny terminal building was a mass of people pushing and shouting, of urgency and noise. My boarding pass was literally thrown at me, as was my passport, which the official hadn't even bothered to open. A list of forbidden hand-luggage items was shoved under my nose: not allowed as carry-on were revolvers, daggers, swords. I shook my head, and the list was snatched away and shown to the next passenger. I don't recall any screening or any security checks. I didn't even notice.

Once the plane came to a halt, groups of airport staff raced towards it, pushing sets of stairs. The doors flew open before the stairs had even been placed outside them; something I had never seen before.

As soon as the passengers from Islamabad appeared at the top of the stairs, they started running down them. I could see around to the other side of the plane, and saw baggage literally being thrown out straight on to the ground. There was no time to get it neatly into baggage carts. An official grabbed my rucksack and ran with it to the baggage compartment, throwing it high into the air, where it vanished from sight.

The outgoing passengers were screaming at the incoming passengers to hurry and get off the plane.

'Clouds are coming!' went up the frantic cry.

Everyone was shoving and pulling each other, although they just stopped short of trying to ascend the narrow stairs when people were still coming down them. I have never been in a conflict zone, but the scene looked to me like refugees fleeing in desperation from some warlord, or people being evacuated after a terrible natural disaster. I was in a daze. I had been shoved to the back of the crowd.

'Please, Madame, run!' one of the airport officials said as he arrived beside me. He tugged the sleeve of my shalwar and ran alongside me to the bottom of the back steps, where passengers were hauling each other into the plane as if they were rescuing drowning people from the water. I raced up the steps and found a seat. Nobody was sitting in their allocated seats – or at least, myself and the man who was already occupying my seat were not. I collapsed into a window seat as the doors slammed shut and the engines began to rev.

That flight from Skardu to Islamabad is the only plane journey I've ever been on where no safety instructions at all were given. Nobody told us how to put on masks or life jackets. The message couldn't be clearer: if we crashed among the glaciers and the mountains and the crevasses and arêtes that we were now flying through and over, nobody would survive.

Instead of a safety announcement, and demonstrations with masks and life jackets, the pilot came on the tannoy and introduced himself. He recited a prayer to the Prophet for a safe journey through a difficult way.

'Inshallah,' he incanted, as I stared down into the landscape I had been looking up at for weeks, and was now finally leaving. It looked different from up here; from this new and startling perspective. I had survived. Whatever happened, I would continue to survive. 'Inshallah,' I breathed.

Thailand
2002

FORTUNA

- goddess of luck,
chance and fate

LUCK. GOOD FORTUNE. Fate. Destiny. Roll of the dice. We navigate our way through the days, for the most part, with blessed unselfconscious ease. The fact that we go out of our doors in the morning and mostly return unscathed in the evening seems a small daily miracle to me. The things that could happen to endanger your life but don't are an incalculable number. You can't think about it, or you would go out of your mind.

By 2002, I had been travelling the world at regular intervals since 1987; some fifteen years. It's 2018 when I write this, so I can add another bundle of years and travels to that tally. Instead of going out your own door every day, going out countless new and different doors in new and different places where you do not know the terrain, people or language is a particular kind of challenge. In all that time, I have been very fortunate. I have never once, while elsewhere, been physically or sexually assaulted, robbed or seriously ill. Those are incredibly lucky odds for all the miles beneath my feet, and I feel charmed to have had this record.

It's not that nothing unpleasant or potentially serious ever happened along the way, though.

In Kathmandu, Nepal, I walked alone back to my guesthouse late at night, turned a corner and saw with horror a pack of three dogs come running towards me. They were barking and snarling with such ferocity they completely cancelled out the sounds of my screaming. I see them still; their teeth bared, gums exposed, their hackles utterly stiff, as they ran around me in ever-tightening circles; wild street dogs that could have rabies. My guesthouse was only metres away, but it might as well have been kilometres. I couldn't think. I could only scream. It was all happening so fast.

The dogs sensed my terror and began to lunge towards me. I was trying to kick them away. I think I was. I don't know what I was doing. I couldn't stop screaming. They were literally running ever smaller rings around me. I had a clear vision of them knocking me to the ground and savaging me with those terrible teeth. Suddenly, the smallest dog lurched in and bit me hard on my right calf; hard enough for its teeth to puncture my skin. In that moment – that nano, split, infinitesimally tiny second – I feared the two larger dogs would also enter the broken circle and start to bite and bite and bite.

I don't know how I did it, but I was suddenly up on a wall, stones in my hand, throwing them at the dogs, still screaming. There were always stones lying around on the Kathmandu streets. I had managed to grab a fistful while simultaneously springing atop this wall. The dogs fled. I stayed on the wall for some time, still unable to stop screaming, still terrified they would come back and attack me again, between the wall and the safety of my guesthouse door.

The result of that experience was five rabies shots and small stones in my pockets at all times ever after when walking alone in faraway places.

Then there was the lampshade in Sri Lanka. I had gone to Sri Lanka because of a book. When I was twenty-six, I read Michael Ondaatje's *Running in the Family*. It entranced me, right from the first sentence: 'What began it all was the bright bone of a dream.' You could either say that sentence doesn't make sense, or else see it as a motif for the rest of the book; a shifting journey of memory, imagination and reality through places both real and imagined.

Running in the Family is a kind of travel memoir about Ondaatje's Sri Lankan family; it was a country he left for England when he was eleven and it was still called Ceylon. Parts of the story are fictionalized. Some chapters are simply poems. Nothing in it is linear, or conventional. It defies being placed in any particular genre, which is one of the reasons I loved it so much, and still do.

What he is exploring are the stories of the family and country he left behind as a child. He returns to Sri Lanka as an adult, to seek out both the place it had once been, Ceylon, and the long-dead family members who had remained in his head. He travelled the same railway journeys his family had taken, went to the houses and racecourses and harbours they had visited. His own family came with him from Canada, where he now lived, and he walked with them through heat and monsoon, continually trying to return to a place no one can ever fully access – the past. He writes so beautifully about all this through so many different styles that the book itself reads like one long surreal and impressionistic dream.

I went to Sri Lanka because of an extravagant, hopeful notion that I too could experience some of the surreality Ondaatje describes. On my first evening, I went walking at sunset on the beach at Negombo. I walked there from my guesthouse through an old churchyard, where a pair of stone angels, their wings broken, stood atop both gatepost pillars. The angels were covered with an ephemeral lattice of cream and yellow frangipani blossoms. When I stopped to look, a wild hog appeared from nowhere and ran to hide behind a gravestone in the graveyard, his ferocious squealing giving away his location.

When I returned to my guesthouse, I hooked up my mosquito net to the lamp on the wall above my bed. It was hot and humid, and I was not wearing any clothes. I woke early in the morning and was at once keen to start the day; my first day in a new country. Impatiently, I jerked the mosquito net. It was hooked over the glass lampshade; a light fitting I had assumed was attached to the wall. It was not.

When I tugged at the mosquito net, it swiftly came falling down. So too did the glass lampshade. It smashed on my forehead. Fragments and shards of glass exploded all over my bare skin. I lay there in shock. Then I became aware of a few things. That my forehead hurt, quite badly. That my naked self was covered with scores of pieces of broken glass. That I was bleeding; blood began to run into one of my eyes.

I lay there immobile for a couple of minutes. I was trying to figure out how to get up without making pieces of glass lodge in my skin; was wondering how many more pieces were on the floor that I might step on in my bare feet. Slowly, carefully, I sat up. There was blood on the white sheet. I began to brush away the glass from my skin. My torso was covered in many scratches, but they were all minor.

I got off the bed and gingerly picked my way across the floor to the bathroom, where there was a mirror. I looked into it with trepidation. I have never had a reason to be vain, but I was a young woman in my twenties then and afraid my face might be permanently damaged. A large open gash high across my forehead was now bleeding a lot. I did not want to think about the fact that my eyes had escaped being lacerated by glass.

I felt a little faint, and held on to the edge of the washbasin for balance. My blood dripped down on its white porcelain.

As if in a daze, I managed to put on some clothes. I took one of the towels from the bathroom, put it under the tap for a while, and held it against my forehead. Then I went to reception, in search of help.

'I think I need a doctor. For stitches,' I managed to say to the astounded man at reception, who called to a colleague.

I wondered if I would pass out. Suddenly I was feeling woozy, and blackness was beginning to crawl in behind my eyes; a sure sign a full-on faint was not far off.

Someone brought me water, and I sat down and put my head between my knees. I began to feel a little better. Someone tapped me gently on the back. It was the man from the reception desk.

'Come, Madame,' he said. He was holding a large umbrella.

I had not even realized it was raining; an early-morning monsoon rain. We stepped out into a blizzard of felled frangipani petals and the sweet scent of jasmine that permeated the air. The rain fell like a collapsing orchestra, playing different sounds on the leaves, the tin roofs, the awnings we were walking among. We walked through the village side by side in the insistent, extraordinary rain, me still holding the wet towel to my forehead, and he tilting the umbrella over me so carefully, so tenderly, so protectively; a human guardian angel sheltering me under a wing, until we reached the doctor's surgery.

The result of that experience is a permanent jagged little scar high on my forehead, and extreme care when hanging a mosquito net ever since.

Then there was the snake in Cambodia. There is always a snake experience somewhere in every country that has snakes.

Mostly, snakes stay away from you. I wasn't really afraid of encountering one, which was good, because I did, from time to time. In Australia, quite often. In Hue in Vietnam, a snake's black head suddenly rising like a startled giraffe from a rice field I was walking in, right beside me. In Laos, coiled up asleep in the sun on a pathway in front of me, when I was walking one morning near Luang Prabang.

At Siem Reap, I had hired a motorbike driver, or 'moto' driver, as they were called, to take me round the temples of Angkor. He had been at the temples a hundred times; a thousand times. Vithu cheerfully drove me to whatever temple I wanted to see, then waited outside while I went to explore, chatting or eating or smoking with the other moto drivers. It was my second afternoon of three days at the temple complex when I arrived at Preah Khan.

I always wore a sunhat, but I had it in my hand that afternoon as I was walking towards the temple. I couldn't make it stay on my head while on the moto. I walked into the jungly entrance of Preah Khan, dreaming as usual, in the hot still afternoon, amazed all over again by the stone carvings I had seen, the apsaras, the friezes, the jigsaw of blocks of stones, the garudas, the nagas, the size and scale of this marvellous place.

Suddenly I heard something thud to the ground just behind me, where I had been walking a moment before. In the same instant, I heard a weird chorus of screaming go up behind me. I turned immediately. What I saw was a snake I later discovered was a green tree pit viper, undulating at speed towards the undergrowth. What I also saw was a group of Japanese tourists, shrieking and running after the snake, cameras pointed.

I ran. Away from the snake. Away from the tourists running after the snake with their cameras. The pit viper had fallen out of the tree at the exact place I had walked underneath a moment – a nano, split, infinitesimally tiny second – previously. If I had passed in that tiny second earlier, the snake would have fallen on my unprotected head and neck, and who knows where it would have gone then. Down the back of my open-necked shirt? Coiled around my neck in an effort to stop falling? Grasped hold of the arm I would instinctively have raised?

Green tree pit vipers usually live in trees, wrapping themselves around branches, until they unexpectedly fall out of one. The one I saw was about half a metre long. They are venomous and, unsurprisingly, due to their everyday habitat, most of their bites to humans are to the neck or face. No pair of boots will protect you from an arboreal snake falling on to your head and neck.

When I was finished exploring Preah Khan, I went back out to find Vithu. I still did not know what kind of snake it had been. I told him the story. I told him the vivid lime green colour of the snake, and that it had fallen out of the tree I was walking under. I expected him to laugh it off. Vithu did not. Instead, he looked at me with an expression of fear.

The result of that experience is that I did not fully enjoy exploring the remainder of Angkor's temples.

I knew what the word tsunami meant long before 2004. I had a postcard with a reproduction of Hokusai's most famous woodblock, *The Great Wave off Kanagawa*; the huge wave falling like a deconstructed mountain. Apparently it doesn't actually depict a tsunami wave, but a tidal wave. No matter what the art experts said, whenever I heard the word tsunami, it was always Hokusai's terrifying, almost fictional, disruption of the ocean that flashed into my head.

Sometimes, in Asia, I stood on piers or beaches and scanned the horizon, the image of a tsunami in my head. What I was always looking for was an unnaturally giant wave. Even though I knew what a tsunami was, I did not then know it is preceded by the tide being violently sucked far, far out. I did not realize I was never on guard for the correct warning signal. The wave appears shortly before it breaks. It had never occurred to me to examine the structure of the Japanese word *tsunami*: *tsu*, harbour; *nami*, wave.

I rarely planned anything when I was travelling, and this proved problematic at Christmas time in Thailand. I discovered that lots of people were arriving from overseas just for the holiday season, so getting accommodation was a whole lot harder and much more expensive than usual. Flights were full, berths on overnight trains were booked out, ferries were crowded. I couldn't settle anywhere; couldn't find a place I felt like staying in.

By the time Christmas came, I had arrived on Koh Phi Phi Don. It's an island close to Koh Phi Phi Leh, which featured in the movie *The Beach*; where you cannot actually stay, just visit by longboat on a day trip. My ferry arrived on the south side of the island, into Ton Sai Bay. The island is shaped like the kind of bone a dog in a cartoon would eat: long and narrow in the middle and raised up on either side. It's a small island, and it was literally a walk of a few minutes from the pier at Ton Sai Bay to Loh Dalam Bay on the north side.

I wandered around, looking for a room close to the beach. Most of the accommodation was full. I crossed over to the northern side of the island and in another complex, which I think was called the Princess, I was offered a bamboo hut on stilts, but it was more than I felt like paying and a bit isolated. I like a buzz, and being near things, especially when I'm alone.

The room I took was a small concrete bungalow at a complex called Charlie's. It was pretty much on the beach, overlooking Loh Dalam Bay.

I have gone over that place so often in my head. The frankly ugly concrete bungalow; one of some twenty-five others. 'Bungalow' is a misnomer; they were all small rooms, built separately from each other. It was so utterly nondescript. The window on the right of the door, a double bed with a languid fan overhead, the door to the bathroom opposite the entrance door, the desk with a mirror over it that I could see myself in when I sat up in bed. It had no charm. The only good thing about it was its proximity to the curving beach.

I stayed at Charlie's right up until New Year's Day. From the list I made at the back of my diary of the books I read along the way, I can see that the first on Koh Phi Phi Don was *When We Were Orphans* by Kazuo Ishiguro, *Cold Mountain* by Charles Frazier, and then *The Glass Palace* by Amitav Ghosh. You read indiscriminately – or at least I did, before technology – literally whatever books you could find, or swap, or buy along the way. It was the first time I had read Ishiguro, and I distinctly recall lying on my bed one afternoon, when I had just finished the book, and trying to shake off the melancholy it had cast over me. I wished I hadn't read it; that I didn't have that indefinable sadness and mannered loss now in my head. I can't recall anything of the plot, other than part of it was set in Shanghai and involved a child mysteriously separated from his parents, but I remember how strange and unsettled it made me feel.

I spent an hour or so every morning lingering over break-fast, writing my diary and looking out over the ocean. I see that beach still; its shallow curve bounded on either side by hills. I read, swam, wandered around the little tourist shops, went on a boat trip snorkelling one day, and did not do much else; was fretting for New Year to be over and go onwards to less crowded places. Sometimes, in the afternoons, I went to the open-air bar at Charlie's, where grainy bootleg movies were shown. Once I watched A *Knight's Tale*, starring the still undead Heath Ledger. In the evenings, if I wanted to be by myself, I went to a bar near the beach, and if I wanted com-pany, I liked to go to a bar called Tintin's, or another called the Reggae Bar.

On New Year's Eve, the staff at Charlie's set up tables and chairs on the beach and ran an expensive buffet dinner for its guests. If you were staying there, the New Year's dinner was a mandatory cost, a practice common at many guesthouses. I shared a table with three Frenchmen, and at midnight we ran laughing into the sea together, fully clothed, while flares and fireworks went off on the beach. I departed the next day, and never again thought about Charlie's or my wholly unre-markable time on Koh Phi Phi Don.

Never thought about it again, that is, until St Stephen's Day, two years later. I woke up to hear the horrific news of the tsunami that had devastated the coast and islands of so many parts of South East Asia. It took some time for the scale of it to register. So many places affected. So many dead. So much devastation. I could barely comprehend what had happened.

There was no social media in 2004, but at the time I was on a Lonely Planet discussion forum called Thorn Tree where people posted questions and answers about travel. I tried to find out what I could about Koh Phi Phi Don, and what had happened there. I had to stop. It was too distressing to read the frantic messages of people trying to locate family and friends who had been there when the wave hit.

It was on the northern side of the island, the beach on Loh Dalam Bay, that I and the three French tourists ran into the sea at midnight; it was here the tsunami came roaring in, destroying, demolishing, killing, drowning, eviscerating.

I could not stop thinking: what happened to all those people working and staying at Charlie's? The women who brought me breakfast every morning? The man who put on the afternoon bootleg videos? The women who swept out the huts? The chefs who cooked the New Year's Eve dinner? The unknown person or couple staying in the hut I had occupied, two years previously? And the people in the other squat concrete bungalows, which would all be full, because it was so hard to get accommodation on the islands at that time of year? I couldn't bear to think about it and yet I could not get it out of my head. When I closed my eyes, I saw again my doomed nondescript room in Charlie's; a coffin in the making.

The truth is, eventually I discovered that almost every one of those people working and staying at Charlie's had died. It was the resort closest to the beach, with the Princess next to it, and was the first place the wave struck.

We almost never know when death will arrive. But it is rare to be able to identify both a particular day in your life and a location where you know that if you had been there on that precise date a certain number of years into the future, you would have died. It seems almost crass to dwell on it when so many people died; when so many others must have been severely traumatized by the sheer randomness of missing the tsunami by a week, a day, an hour.

And yet, I do occasionally think about being at Charlie's on that Thai island for Christmas 2002. It's human nature to wonder how we have managed to survive as long as we already have; to regard with shock from a safe distance how some sinister trapdoor can open unexpectedly beneath us due to fate, coincidence and a terrifying act of nature.

Since I left Koh Phi Phi Don, I have lost peers and friends of different ages to death in unexpected, painful and traumatic scenarios. More than one to suicide. Two to cancer. One to a rare reaction to a certain illness. One younger than me to heart failure when she lay down to sleep as usual one Saturday evening; a sleep she never awoke from, leaving behind a small son and stunned husband.

I recall exactly where I was when I received the news about each of them. The most difficult memory of all is from the first day of my Christmas holiday in 2011. I was delivering cards mid-morning to neighbours in our little cul-de-sac when my phone rang. I was walking up a flight of stone steps at the time, phone in one hand, ready to push an envelope through the next letterbox; idly figuring out which dress I would wear to a party later that day.

The call was from my close friend and colleague, Róisín. She was crying so hard that initially I couldn't make out what she was saying, but I finally registered the name of a fellow beloved friend and editor, and the word 'dead'. She had been found in the sea the previous night and died a few hours later in hospital.

The news of that particular, utterly tragic and devastating death remains one of the worst shocks I've ever had. I went into a weird, intense, automatic zone for at least a month, unable to believe or process what had happened. The funeral was on Christmas Eve. I knew the only way I could get through it was by working, because my professional self would then have to mercifully take over.

Together with another friend and colleague, Kathy, I volunteered to report on the funeral. On a bone-cold Christmas Eve morning, I stood outside Newman University Church on St Stephen's Green as the mourners arrived. As I gathered tributes, I felt that the notebook I was fiercely holding on to was doubling as a shield to protect from any more damage. People I knew were trying to sympathize with me on the loss of a colleague that the whole of literary Dublin held dear, but I didn't want to hear their condolences: it would have broken me entirely. I cut off their sympathies mid-sentence and grimly collected names and quotes for my article instead.

I had learned almost everything of value I knew about journalism from the person we were gathered together to mourn; my inspirational and trusted mentor, who had had such warmth and generosity of spirit and had always been so joyously full of abundant life. She periodically dropped treasured jewels of insight on my desk while passing: she was someone perpetually in movement. In one of these rushed and random pilgrimages to my desk, she had instructed me always to listen carefully while interviewing someone for what she described as *la ligne donnée* – the given line.

It's the sentence that identifies the core and nub and *raison d'être* of everything; whether a person, a situation, or a story. She taught me that you have to keep going with the work and the interview until you hear someone say 'la ligne donnée'; but the true skill is in learning to recognize this utterance and knowing with certainty when you hear it. Then, you analyse what it means and why it is important, and use it as a depth-sounder to report further and yet further; something I try very hard to do in every long-form story I work on. To be reporting on my cherished editor's funeral that day was very close to unbearable, but someone had to do it, and I knew that it was the best possible gesture I could offer to her bereaved family.

Kathy and I had made a pact to stay together while we wrote up our pieces; to take care of each other as best we could during this dreadful self-imposed task. After the funeral, we went back to the newspaper's office, festooned with its ridiculous festive tinsel, deserted except for the security guard. Her daughter briefly arrived with sandwiches and coffee neither of us had any appetite for. The two of us sat numbly at adjacent desks, writing while people passed under the windows four floors beneath, drunkenly singing Christmas carols.

It was Kathy, reporting from inside the church, who identified and pulled out the note-perfect *ligne donnée* of the day. It came from the eulogy our friend's husband gave the congregation about the legacy his wife was leaving. 'The great enterprise that was her life, the stardust she scattered every single day.'

So many of us gathered in that church had experienced her stardust; it glitters on me still.

It is a brutal cliché in a profession that abhors clichés, but I have learned over time that life is very short and very precious and sometimes horrifyingly truncated for reasons that make no sense. My late editor's photograph stands on my desk at work: it's been there since the day I returned to the office after her death, and it will remain there until the day I leave the building for the last time. Sometimes I look at it and wonder what advice she would impart about whatever story I am currently working on, or whatever personal dilemma is presently facing me.

I'll never know the answers to those questions. All I can do is appreciate my luck in having known and learned from her, and having survived thus far in my own life, and vow afresh never to take for granted the momentous fact of simply being alive. I cannot imagine how those people who survived or only just escaped the Asian tsunami that destroyed Charlie's and all those unthinkably many other places navigated their way through life afterwards, but I am certain most of them never again took their lives for granted.

There is a form of Chinese calligraphy, *dishu*, that involves writing on surfaces with a paintbrush dipped in water. The characters briefly glisten into visibility, and then vanish; a body of words disappearing into the ground. Our lives are as ephemeral as words written in water.

Japan
2003

KINTSUKUROI

– to repair with gold

THE SHINKANSEN BULLET train from Tokyo to Kakunodate was going so fast it felt like a plane perpetually taxiing on the runway before take-off. It was travelling at such speed that the handwriting in my diary was turning out shaky and uneven. We were flying past conifer forests and Japanese maple trees and snowy mountains. I was writing about the things I had seen in the Tokyo National Museum two days before.

I had been fascinated to observe a succession of men standing with intense concentration before displays of swords in the Honkan building, the main part of the sprawling museum. There was an entire gallery given over to swords, some of them once used by samurai. To my utterly untrained eye, they all looked more or less the same, but clearly they were not.

I had once changed planes at Amsterdam's Schiphol airport with a colleague en route to an assignment in Asia, and we had gone for sashimi and beer to a sushi place on the airport's concourse. It wasn't a fancy place, or even very large; more a kind of diner set-up, with high stools at a counter. We camped out there for almost two hours while waiting for our flight.

For that entire time, a man worked solely on sharpening the blade of one particular knife. He had been at it when we arrived, so who knows for how long he had already been working on it. He never even looked up at us. He was totally focused on his work. He had some kind of whetstone, and every now and then he stopped, tested the blade's edge with his finger and spent some time staring at the knife, carefully turning it over and over in his hand, regarding the edge from every angle before returning to his minutely precise grinding.

I was transfixed by his dedication and wished I could stay there and keep watching, but our onward flight was called, and we had to go, leaving him bent over the same knife, still at his seemingly unending task. It had the drama and intensity of performance theatre. That was just a routine modern knife in an ordinary sushi place in an airport. Looking into the glass cases in Tokyo's flagship museum where historically important swords were displayed, I could scarcely imagine the levels of skilled craftsmanship and the number of hours necessary in honing blades for samurai.

The displays I had spent the most time looking at in the Tokyo museum were of decorative arts; lacquer work, mostly. Every time I thought I had seen the most exquisite of pieces, the next cabinet yielded something even more stunning. There were writing boxes and cosmetic boxes and tea caddies, but what I was struggling to try and write as the shinkansen arrowed northwards through Honshu, was a description of how exceptionally beautiful these objects were.

The lacquerware was sometimes red, a deep sealing-wax red colour, but mainly black. Black with variations of gold and silver decoration. One of the eighteenth-century writing boxes I had looked at was from the Edo period, decorated with golden grasses and mother-of-pearl inlaid flowers. Although the box was eighteenth century, the technique of sprinkled gold designs, called maki-e – so the museum information boards had told me – dated from the eighth century.

Craftsmen had used gold and silver leaf, gold and silver pigments and mother-of-pearl inlays from China to create the illusion of three dimensions. As I moved from cabinet to cabinet, waves and boats and mountains and birds and flowers and temples came alive in their ancient golden glory.

Eventually, I moved on to ceramics. The tea bowls and plates and vases were so delicate and so old. I tried to imagine people deep in the past eating and drinking from these vessels, or arranging flowers in vases destined to long outlive them, regarded by people like me, existing in a world so utterly different from theirs: one of air travel and technology and globalization. It almost hurt my head to think of this museum, as I did of every museum I visited, as a time capsule to the past.

Then, I noticed various pieces that looked different in some way. Beautiful plates and bowls mysteriously veined here and there with gold. A plate with red hollyhocks on a blue background partially rimmed with a golden edge. I looked more closely, puzzled. The gold parts in each piece were irregular, random; not part of the pattern.

And so, I came across *kintsukuroi*, or 'golden joinery'. This is the Japanese art of repairing broken ceramics with lacquer mixed with powdered gold or silver and understanding that the piece is more beautiful for having been mended. The cracks are thus highlighted, as in the gold rim on the hollyhock plate. The repair work is the opposite of usual mending, where you try to make the joins look invisible. The Japanese aesthetic sees the fact of an object being broken as a transition in the life of the piece, not an ending of its existence or cessation of its original purpose.

It was all this I was trying to record in my diary as the train travelled northwards, towards Kakunodate.

*

I'm not sure what exactly drew me to Kakunodate. Partly distance. I had a seven-day Japan Rail Pass, and I intended to use the hell out of it, and cover as much territory as possible. Kakunodate was far north of Tokyo, so I was already getting good value for money. Partly because I liked the sound of the samurai wooden houses I had read about in my guidebook, especially after having looked at the swords and warrior armour in the museum.

On most trips I winged it when it came to accommodation, but Japan was different. For a start, mine had been the only rucksack on the carousel at Narita Airport. There just weren't many other tourists. The country was very expensive. Also, I was finding the language a real difficulty in a way I usually didn't. Very few people spoke English, and I definitely didn't speak any Japanese.

So the previous day, my last in Tokyo, I had gone to a tourist information centre and with the help of the official there, pre-booked my accommodation for the next week. The man at the tourist centre had made all the calls for me, and then presented me with a sheaf of paperwork: maps of the various locations and the names and addresses of the places. I was to pay on arrival.

I wanted as many different experiences as possible, so my reservations included a monastery in Takayama; a hostel located on the top two floors of a skyscraper in Hiroshima; and a ryokan, a traditional Japanese inn, in Kyoto. Tonight's accommodation in Kakunodate was to be in a minshuku, a family-run B & B.

I had chosen the Takimoto minshuku based entirely on the guidebook's recommendation. 'An old house 15 minutes on foot from the station. Excellent meals are served around an irori (open hearth). The owner believes that beer and sake should flow freely and guests are seated next to each other so there's less isolation and more chat.'

I was the only tourist alighting at Kakunodate, which was much colder than it had been in Tokyo, 600 kilometres south. It was afternoon, and I figured I'd drop off my rucksack and then explore. First, I had to get orientated. My sense of direction is appalling. I get lost everywhere I go, including Dublin, where I've lived the longest of anywhere. Before smartphones and the slightly judgemental lady who now guides me to my destination via Google Maps, I routinely built in getting-lost time on every country assignment I did.

So when I could not find the minshuku, into which I was booked for the night, I assumed it was because I was yet again lost. I tramped up and down the streets of Kakunodate, searching for Takimoto, but it wasn't there. After a full hour of wandering, and looking from all angles at the map that the man in the tourist centre had given me, I eventually found it. I had actually passed it at least twice, but it hadn't registered with me, because it was closed. Closed, as in not in business. Shut. Ceased operating.

Flummoxed, I stood outside the shut door. Had I not heard the man in Toyko make all those calls, booking my accommodation? I looked again at the piece of paper. I had the right name and the right address, but it was now clear that this was not the place I would be staying in tonight, eating an excellent meal around an open fire with fellow tourists, and knocking back the free-flowing beer and sake as we merrily exchanged our stories.

I grew up in a house full of newspapers. Each day, we took the *Irish Times* and the *Irish Press*. Each week, we took the *Clare*

Champion, the *Limerick Leader*, and *Kerry's Eye*. Each Sunday, we took the *Sunday Press, The Observer* and the *Sunday Times*. I read the Asterix and Peanuts and Doonesbury cartoons and the television schedules, and looked at the photographs, and flicked through the magazine sections. Everything else was beyond me. As a child, it was normal to live in a household with eighteen newspapers a week passing through it: something close to unthinkable today.

The section I always commandeered on Sundays was the *Sunday Times Magazine*. I did not know it then, but the 1970s was a glorious era for photojournalism. The magazine carried many superb picture essays. Sometimes I kept them, because I wanted to keep looking at them. I was always pulling out things that intrigued me from newspapers and magazines; something I still do to this day. I cut out a picture essay on the rooms that Anne Frank had occupied in Amsterdam's Prinsengracht while in hiding. It was mainly shadows and details; a brilliant and frightening mood piece.

One spring Sunday in 1978 when I was twelve, I opened the 'A Life in the Day Of' column, which always appeared on the inside back page of the magazine. It was – and remains – a column in which people who are usually in the public eye tell a reporter about a typical day in their life. The personality who was to be featured the following week was the designer Laura Ashley.

The person featured that Sunday was neither in the public eye, nor well known. Her name was Mary Philpott. She was an ordinary member of the public, who had written and submitted her own story to the paper. The headline at the top of the piece read: 'Mary Philpott, aged 55, who describes herself as a derelict, wrote to us about her life.'

There was an atmospheric portrait of Mary, taken at her home. Sitting behind a black manual typewriter, elbows on the table, hands clasped under her chin, she was looking straight at the camera with a piercing expression. The room was dimly lit. A gas heater was visible, and an oval mirror over a mantelpiece, which displayed three clocks, each showing a different time. The caption under the photograph read, 'Born in Brockley, London. Spent the war years in a local radio and valve factory, and later went into personnel work. Left employment in 1953 to take care of invalid mother, and, latterly, widower father. Both parents now dead.'

I read the piece. Then I read it again. Then I cut it out. No journalist could ever have told Mary's story better. It was a magnificent piece of writing; so superlative that it even spoke to a twelve-year-old living in a different country. It was told with devastating clarity, in an utterly compelling voice. It began:

'I am a single woman and live in an old rented terraced house in a down-at-heel street in Wallington, Surrey. I am totally alone, except for my cat Tosca, who, like me, is one of today's rejects . . .

'I go to the shops, where I buy a tin of cat food, and, if I can afford it, a tin of vegetable soup for my own dinner. Fortunately, I am vegetarian, so not having the money to buy meat does not worry me unduly, although it would be nice to be able to buy luxuries occasionally, like cakes, fruit, particularly bananas, or a strong piece of Cheddar . . .

'I've been virtually penniless since my father died, some two years ago. My mother, whom I loved dearly, died in 1968. I still mourn her and remember her with absolute love . . .

'One of the not inconsiderable blessings of tea is that it does serve to deaden the appetite . . .

'In the afternoon I go to my local library. In the winter it is warm there and in the summer it's a place to go, a transient escape. I've had no holiday since 1961 and I like to look at the travel books and dream . . .

'I'm not a great conversationalist, which again is fortunate for me, for from the time I get up until I retire, I doubt if I say more than half-a-dozen words to anyone. I've no friends, and there is just no point in talking anyway . . .

'Some years ago I was able to buy myself a record player, and this I've hung onto grimly, although almost all my other personal possessions have been sold. My evenings are usually spent in the company of Mozart's Third Violin Concerto . . .

'I have clung, too, with equal tenacity, to my weekly copy of the *Sunday Times*, which I cannot imagine being without. My other indulgence is my treasured typewriter, an ancient Royal model which I found languishing in a junk-shop some years ago. I bought it, lovingly cleaned, oiled and generally refurbished it, thus I can sit back and type little efforts like this, partly to assuage the dreadful monotony and poverty of my existence, and partly to try and convince myself I'm not really on the scrap heap. Most probably, though, I set this down so there will be some record that I exist at all. Sometimes I doubt it myself . . . '

I have just reread this piece. I still have the clipping. I'm looking at it now. I pasted it into a scrapbook long ago. When I first read it in 1978, I found Mary Philpott's story harrowing. Her loneliness came across so powerfully. Her life seemed so pitifully small. She was surviving on tinned food, and the anonymous shelter of a public library and an aspiration to write: to have her voice heard, to be acknowledged. I thought it was the saddest thing I had ever read.

*

Once I realized the minshuku that I thought had been booked for me in Tokyo was closed, I had to make a decision about time. The afternoon was wearing on, and I was anxious not to lose the chance to explore; to see the samurai houses and to wander around the town. It was winter, and the daylight would fade away in the next couple of hours. I was due to leave on the precisely timetabled 7.21 a.m. train the next day for my next destination (I was definitely getting value from my Japan Rail Pass), and did not want my entire time in Kakunodate to be swallowed up with the quest for accommodation.

So I decided to explore first, and then seek somewhere to stay later.

There was a specific district in the small town where the samurai houses were located. In the spring there are lots of tourists, because of the old houses set against the flowering cherry blossom. The trees were bare now and most of the houses were closed. There was an avenue with dark wooden houses and carved pitched roofs. They stood sternly facing each other from behind tall fences. The gates to each house were closed. It didn't seem as if anyone lived there. An unseen dog suddenly barked out of nowhere, a huge growling, snarling kind of bark, which startled me. There was the strangest and most unnerving atmosphere in the place.

There was nobody out at all, except me. Snow still lay on the ground and on the roofs, and the sky was a peculiar shade of grey. After the frenetic urban chaos of four days in Tokyo, the resolute quiet of Kakunodate was like another culture shock. Years later, when I saw the Hulu production of *The Handmaid's Tale*, I puzzled over what the austere avenue of gated houses in Gilead reminded me of. It was that deserted winter street of samurai houses in Japan.

Only a couple of shops were open. They sold items made from cherry bark; mostly trays, tea caddies and caddy scoops; an art called kabazaiku. The cherry bark glowed with rich colours of amber and chestnut and sienna. Some had cherry blossom flowers inlaid in marquetry over their lids. I picked a few up wistfully. They evoked memories of some of the beautiful things I had seen in the Tokyo museum, where there was a whole gallery devoted to tea-ceremony objects. I bought a tea scoop; a small piece of curved cherry bark that resembled an ancient dugout canoe.

It was dark when I left the shop; the owner locked the door behind me as I left. I went to stand under a street light and consulted the guidebook. Snow was starting to fall. I hadn't an idea where to go, except I hoped it wouldn't cost a fantastic sum of money, which so many things in Japan did.

My book listed only two other minshukus. I eventually located one of them, but nobody responded to my knock on the door, and there were no lights on inside. It was now much colder, and the snow was turning to an unpleasant wet sleet. The second minshuku was at the end of a long, long street. The town faded away behind me as I walked. Finally, I stood outside an anonymous door and rang the bell.

Over time, I have realized that when something traumatic happens, I go silent. Words are my profession, but in bad times, I can't come up with any. During a very, very, very bad time some years ago after a relationship break-up, I took a few days' holiday. I had had no difficulty in continuing to work normally. In fact, I daily welcomed focusing on the structure of research and interviews and writing: work was my safe and familiar anchor in a moiling sea, where I never missed a deadline.

But in my personal life, I was not functioning very well. It was then that I went to Sligo on the train by myself, and checked into a hotel in the town. I had not told anyone where I was going.

The effort of taking the train west and having to compose myself in public had exhausted me. I did not want to go outside the room. Although my first act in any hotel room is always to rearrange the curtains, pulling them back to allow as much light in as possible, on this occasion, I drew them. It was still daylight. I lay on the hotel bed in the dim afternoon in a daze. I love to read, but this time I couldn't get beyond a few sentences. Eventually, I turned on the television. The Winter Olympics had started. A young woman skater in fluttering lavender tulle and sequins flew across the ice like a marvellous fairy. I could not stop watching her. It was the purest of mindless balm.

For the next three days, I remained in my room, the television permanently tuned to the Winter Olympics. I ordered room service, put a Do Not Disturb sign on the door, and did not open the curtains. Housekeeping left fresh towels outside my door, and once, the concierge called the room, presumably to check I was still alive. The Winter Olympics were happening in a different time zone, so whenever the ice skating came on, I watched it. When coverage switched to another sport, I slept.

I had close friends living not far away from Sligo, whom at some point I eventually called. They were horrified to hear I was staying in a hotel. They asked me to come and stay with them. I said no. They called back, and invited me to join them that night for dinner out of town; at a friend's house in rural Leitrim. I said no. I was privately regretting that I had contacted them at all. They insisted. In the end, I gave in, and said yes.

Their friend lived in an old stone cottage in the country-side. There was a fire, and stew, and red wine, and rainbow-coloured candles burning on the table, and lots of banter. It was an evening I usually would have thoroughly enjoyed, but I simply wasn't present. I wished I was back in the hotel room, mindlessly watching triple axels and toe loops and lutzes. I said very little all night. I've never met our host since. He must have thought I was desperately rude. Afterwards, I could never bring myself to enquire.

When the evening ended, my friends arranged a taxi to take me to Sligo. I sat in the back seat and didn't talk to the driver. Both of these things are considered social faux pas when in a taxi in rural Ireland. I didn't care. We reached Lough Gill, where the Lake Isle of Innisfree is. I stared out the window at the winter darkness, wondering how I would ever begin to adjust to life without the man I had loved and understood so completely; the man who had loved and understood me in the exact same way. We had believed that our relationship was unbreakable, but the terrible truth of life is, nothing is unbreakable. And this is what heartbreak now felt like; this broken person I had become.

There was no one else out on the road. We drove along-side the edge of the lake. A full moon suddenly emerged from behind a cloud and illuminated the entire surface of the lake with a quivering silvery light. It was so unexpected and so beautiful that it fleetingly shook me out of my trance. Then the clouds claimed the moon back, and we left the lake behind us and headed in towards Sligo.

On the train back to Dublin the next day, I found myself thinking about that lake glimmering like shook foil in the moonlight. I could not get it out of my head. As we rattled past Boyle and Longford and Enfield, I gradually realized why. I had felt a brief rush of joy in that moment. It was the first time since my relationship had ended some months previously that I had felt anything other than despair. Something instinctive in me had responded, and in that response, I knew I was not dead on the inside after all, no matter how much it felt like that.

When we reached Connolly Station, and my fellow passengers scattered on to the platform and beyond in search of transport home, I held on to that memory tightly. It helped me believe that, one day in the future, I would again be capable of joy; joy that would last longer than a moment. That some kind of *kintsukuroi* repair work would one day mend my fragmented heart.

In Kakunodate, nobody answered the door of the minshuku I was standing outside. But unlike the other one I had tried, here there were lights on inside. I rang and knocked several times. Something struck me. I tried the door handle. It opened, and I stepped inside.

'Konnichiwa!' I called. I had precisely three words of Japanese; those for hello, thank you, and goodbye. Nobody appeared. I was standing with my rucksack in what looked like somebody's home; a home that was meant to be a B & B where I might or might not be spending the night. For the first time that day, I felt a stab of anxiety. Where was I going to stay that night? How could I make myself understood? Why did these things always seem to happen to me: how could I have thought back in Tokyo that everything was sorted for the next week about where I would stay, yet now I was figuring out everything for myself again? Was this going to happen every-where else I turned up in Japan?

I didn't think it was appropriate for me to remain waiting in someone's house while it was unoccupied, even if it was meant to be a minshuku. I took out my notebook, went to the vocabulary section at the back of the guidebook, and painfully cobbled together a couple of basic sentences, to the effect that my name was Rosita and I was a tourist from Ireland hoping to stay the night.

I left the note with its poorly written message on top of my rucksack, which I then left in the middle of the hallway, where it could not possibly be missed by someone opening the front door on their return. I went back outside again and continued to wander around the streets of Kakunodate in the dark, searching for a hotel as a potential back-up, but could not find one.

Along with the eighteen newspapers that passed through our house each week as I was growing up, I was used to seeing my father lean against the fridge at 1 p.m. each day to listen to the news. The radio in the kitchen was located atop the fridge, and he was listening closely to the One O'Clock News on RTÉ Radio. At 9 p.m., he ritually watched the television evening news, and if I was in the room, I had to be completely quiet for its duration. There was a much larger radio in my parents' bedroom, which remained on all night, tuned to BBC Radio 4: on my nocturnal visits to the bathroom, I could hear posh British accents murmuring softly from under their door.

I never consciously listened to the news – it was dull, and went on far too long – but certain things still found their way to my consciousness. Like the appeals. It was always summer when the appeals went out on the radio.

'And now, we have a special appeal to members of the public,' the announcement would start, and my attention was caught. What followed was always a variation on this: Mr and Mrs X, or the X Family from the US, or England, or 'the continent', were on holiday in Ireland, driving a rented car. The car registration would then be called out, and its make, model and colour. Members of the public were asked to be on the lookout for this car. If they saw it, they were to tell the occupants to 'contact home, for an urgent message'.

What could those messages be? I would wonder, thrilled by the idea that people like me were being asked to be on the lookout for certain cars. Sometimes, I wrote down these registration numbers, peering carefully at the cars I saw on my way back and forth from school for the next day or two. As a child, I very badly wanted the self-importance of knocking on a car window and solemnly informing the unwitting occupants that they had to contact home for an urgent message.

I didn't realize until much later that the nature of these 'urgent messages' would invariably have been entirely grim. They meant that, back home, some close family member was either seriously ill, or dead. In the era before smartphones and social media and the internet, the only way of contacting people on holiday in another country during a family crisis was by appealing to the country's police force and state media to issue these messages to the public.

As I wandered the streets of Kakunodate on that winter's night, I began to feel irrational anxiety that bad things were happening back in Ireland to someone in my family; that someone, right now, might possibly be looking for me. How,

I found myself thinking, would anyone ever find me if an emergency arose, when I hardly knew where I was myself? Did anyone I knew even know I was in Japan at present, let alone in which town? If I couldn't be located, did I in fact exist? Feeling unexpectedly vulnerable, I eventually made my way back to the house in which I had left my rucksack.

This time, the hosts, a man and woman, were at home. They were sitting in their living room, staring with evident suspicion at my rucksack, which they had moved in from the hall. It was less than eighteen months after 9/11 and it some-how had not occurred to me to consider that the owners of the B & B, arriving back to find a stranger's bag in their house without the stranger present, might possibly be freaked out.

There followed an awkward and not entirely pleasant few minutes, when I had absolutely no idea what was being said, except I was guessing from the tone of the voices that they were far from happy to have me as an unannounced guest. I had already decided that, whether they liked it or not, I was staying here tonight. I showed them my passport and smiled a lot. I produced a sheaf of yen. I pointed out the name and address of their B & B in my guidebook and kept on smiling.

In the end, the man took my yen and the woman indicated that I was to follow her. She showed me into a spartan room with sliding doors that contained only a sideboard, tatami mats and a window with sliding paper blinds. Then she came back with a pile of bedding and a cherry bark tray with a pot of green tea, a tea bowl, and nothing else on it. She indicated I was to make a bed on the mat, and put her hands under one cheek, closing her eyes and tilting her head sideways. It was not even 8 p.m. Was she telling me to go to sleep?

I went back out again, leafed through my vocabulary pages, and asked haltingly if there was anywhere I could get something to eat. There was more angry-sounding conversation from the two of them. I stood there in hungry mortification.

The man of the house drove me in silence to a restaurant yet further into the suburbs and away from the town. He indicated he would wait outside for me while I ate and then drive me back. I was excruciated at the way my arrival had disrupted their entire evening. I was the only person in the restaurant. I swallowed at speed my miso soup and stir-fried beef and rice, and, within twenty minutes, was again back in my little room, staring at the pile of bedding.

I made up a bed, and lay down hours earlier than I usually did, and tried to read a book, but couldn't concentrate. My inability to communicate, the sour hosts, the whole counter-narrative to the happy, convivial evening I had hoped for when I'd set out from Tokyo that morning, had made me sad. I felt lonely. I set my alarm, turned off the light and lay there, unable to sleep, listening to the sound of the snow sliding off the roof and water running in the gutters.

Four years after I went to Japan, I came across a book in a charity shop called *Deadline Sunday: Life in the Week of the Sunday Times*, by Brian MacArthur. Published in 1991, it described an era when print newspapers were radically different from today. I have a collection of books relating to journalism, and bought it, curious to discover how the *Sunday Times* had operated in 1991. The introduction stated that 15 million British people bought a newspaper every day, and on Sundays 'so avid is their appetite for something to read, 17 million buy one of the 10 national Sunday papers'. Those were the days.

When I got home, I leafed through the book. My hand stopped on page 156, and so too did my breath. There was Mary Philpott looking up at me; the same photograph from 1978. Mary's article was reproduced in full. At the end of her piece, there was this:

> Of all the 400 or so *Life in the Days*, Mary Philpott's aroused the greatest response from readers: hundreds of letters to us and to her, presents for herself and Tosca, invitations, offers of friendship, holidays, jobs. She was overwhelmed, thrilled, and felt she could at last 'overcome that sense of being lost, of being non-existent'. The local newspaper and a couple of publishers got in touch with her; a professor of English wrote that he hoped we realised she was a born writer . . .

There was an update too, from 1991: 'She writes (still from her old address) to say as she now qualifies for an old age pension she is not in such desperate straits financially.'

I read this and felt so happy to know something good had come out of the article for her. Some *kintsukuroi* had happened for her too. It shouldn't have surprised me, from what I now know about the power a beautifully told and authentic story has to move readers, but when I was twelve, I knew nothing of how journalism worked. Some sharp-eyed editor had immediately spotted her talent when the unsolicited piece came in.

It's now forty years since I first read Mary Philpott's story and fifteen since that lonely night in Kakunodate, and I have never forgotten either experience. When I returned to Mary's story just now, her age registered fully with me for the first time. I am only a couple of years younger than she was in 1978. Back then, I didn't even notice what age she was.

Now I am so close to her in age; here now in that separate universe that was once so far away when I looked at it through the telescope of childhood. I don't like ageing. I really don't. Who does? But having experienced people close to me dying long before their time, I know it is a privilege just to be alive, no matter what your age is.

Somewhere in my head after I read Mary Philpott's story as a child was a deep fear that this would be my own life one day. That I would be lonely and friendless and trapped within the parameters of a pathetically tiny world. I couldn't then distinguish between temporal situations that make us all lonely, such as my peculiar night in a small Japanese town fifteen years ago, and the viscerality of an entire life shaped by poverty and solitariness.

But what I did know at the time was how her story made me feel. It was the first time I knew, without ever understanding why, that powerfully written words could be a catalyst for emotion; to being moved, to feeling empathy for someone else. I did not know it then, but, somewhere in my consciousness, Mary Philpott's story showed me how important journalism could be in telling the universal, unforgettable stories of ordinary people.

Antarctica
2007

QUIDDITY

- the essence
of a thing

ONE CHRISTMAS, I had gone for three weeks to New Zealand. As I had travelled out from Auckland, down through the South Island, and on to Stewart Island, the country's most southerly land mass, I had gradually become aware of the presence of Antarctica. Antarctica was firmly located in the consciousness of New Zealand; a kind of gravitational pull further southwards on the imagination that I found both compelling and unexpectedly stirring.

For the first time in my life, I heard people talking casually about Antarctica. The country has a research base there, the Scott Base, where they have been since 1957. People I encountered knew others who had either worked on the base or were out there now. It seemed fantastical to me that people had Antarctica as a word in their ordinary, everyday lexicon. The man sitting beside me on the bus to Invercargill had actually worked on the Scott Base for a winter season; something to do with measuring data from glaciers and water.

'What was it like?' I enquired inanely, desperate to know more.

'Bloody cold,' he said, laughing. 'And boring.' Then he settled back into his seat and fell asleep, while I resisted an urge to poke him awake and grill him thoroughly about life at the South Pole.

At Invercargill's Southland Museum, I lingered for a long time in a permanent exhibition called 'Beyond the Roaring 40°s'. The name was a reference to the high winds found in the southern hemisphere, usually between latitudes of the 'Roaring 40' and 50 degrees, which were known as 'Furious'.

The exhibition explained that due to the fact that ships had so frequently been wrecked in these waters, shipwreck huts had been established on some of the Subantarctic Islands that lay between New Zealand and Antarctica. The huts contained items to aid survival – tools, dry food, fishing tackle – until the next passing whaling ship would routinely call to see if any castaways had survived a known shipwreck and needed rescuing. Such routine calls could be more than two years apart.

There was an actual castaway hut in the museum, along with some of the items shipwrecked men would have found in it. This hut had survived intact with all its contents, because it had never been used. I stared at it for a long time, imagining it on the island it had been salvaged from. It seemed to me as storied an object in its own way as Shackleton's famous hut on Cape Royds in Antarctica, where he and his exploration party had stayed during the *Discovery* expedition.

The castaway hut was a crude wooden construction, like a tall garden shed, the planks of wood flensed grey by weather. It had stood for years on a rocky subantarctic island awaiting men who never came. Along with the knives and implements were clothes intended for sailors who had first endured shipwreck, then managed to swim to shore and find this hut, while processing the fact that they would be cast away on the island for months, perhaps years. The clothes left for them were brown three-piece tweed suits.

What kind of mind, I wondered, fascinated, could possibly have thought that a tweed waistcoat was a necessary item of clothing for a shipwrecked sailor? Had castaway sailors been rescued after years, wearing ragged tweed suits? Had any of them actually put on the waistcoats?

The following day, I took the ferry from the wonderfully named Bluff across the Foveaux Strait to Stewart Island. I stood out on deck for the rough crossing, staring up at the sky in a trance. Gradually, I noticed an enormous white bird gliding far above us, its wings tilted sideways, as if it was leaning on air.

'Mollymawk,' the woman standing next to me said, also looking skywards.

'Mollymawk?'

'Part of the albatross family. Smaller ones. It's the wandering albatrosses are the biggest,' she explained briskly, while I stared upwards, feeling as if I was seeing the dove from Noah's Ark.

Then I noticed they were everywhere, these mollymawk albatrosses, balancing in the air on the tip of their long white wings. I had never seen an albatross before.

To me, the albatross was a bird that belonged in Antarctic waters, and in the haunting, atmospheric lines of Coleridge's *Rime of the Ancient Mariner*, bits and pieces of which gradually came back into my head as I stood there, staring up at the mollymawks.

> *And through the drifts the snowy clifts*
> *Did send a dismal sheen:*
> *Nor shapes of men nor beasts we ken—*
> *The ice was all between . . .*

At length did cross an Albatross,
Thorough the fog it came . . .

On Stewart Island, someone had made a sign and put it up near the pier at Oban, where the ferry docked. LAST STOP BEFORE ANTARCTICA, it read.

For years, I had thought about Antarctica, a place that seemed as remote as the moon, and equally unlikely as a place that I would ever get to. It fascinated me, although I wasn't sure exactly why. It was partly the remoteness of it, and the stories I'd read of the explorers who had gone there, some of whom had never come back, as if they'd fallen down some arcane well. It was partly the thought of a landscape that was in every way the reverse of the landscape I knew; almost like the negative of a photograph. After I had been to New Zealand, I began to plan a journey there.

I arrived in Ushuaia, at the far south of Tierra del Fuego, Argentina, in early November 2007. I'd been travelling round South America for some time, on a six-month unpaid leave of absence from my job. I had a reason for arriving in Ushuaia early in November. The previous year, I had become aware of the fact that if you turned up there on spec at the beginning of the cruising season, there was a good chance of getting a 'last-minute' ticket for a vastly reduced price on a tourist ship that was going out to Antarctica. The thing is, I had no idea what that price might be.

The pull of Antarctica was very strong in Ushuaia. There was a piercingly cold wind funnelling through the narrow streets of the small city, which had a Nordic feel to it, with brightly coloured tin roofs, and dramatic snow-covered mountains to the north. The souvenir shops were full of penguins. Stuffed penguins of every size looked blankly out at me from behind glass. A rookery of them. A waddle of them. A huddle of cuddles. The penguin motif dominated the souvenirs: in addition to the stuffed toys, the birds were on T-shirts, key rings, mugs, tea towels, sweatshirts, in snow-domes and on posters and clocks and bags and umbrellas.

I walked around the modest grid of streets, feeling like a diviner whose unseen hazel twig was tugging me down to the harbour, where a bilingual sign painted on a wall overlooking the water declared like a haiku in words metre-high: *Ushuaia, End of the World, Beginning of Everything.*

Lovely as remote Ushuaia was, it was the unseen continent that lay beyond the Beagle Channel that was the true draw of the place. This was the most popular departure port to Antarctica for the tourist ships. It was the beginning of the summer season, which ran roughly from the start of November to the end of February; a window of weather when ships could get through the ice. The first ships of the season had gone out only that week.

The majority of the ships embarking from Ushuaia that season were going out for ten days at a time, and it was one of these boats I was hoping to get out on. It takes two and a half days to enter Antarctic waters from the South American archipelago where Ushuaia is located, crossing the Drake Passage en route. The next five days are spent cruising around the Weddell Sea and making landings around the far northwest of the Antarctic peninsula, and then the return journey begins. There are longer cruises of up to three weeks that take in South Georgia and the Falklands, and they are accordingly a lot more expensive.

The following morning, I made my rounds of the six travel agents in Ushuaia that represented cruise ship companies. After two agencies, I had learned a lot. I had started to learn the things you can only really discover once you arrive in a place, no matter how intensively you might mine Google for information in advance. I had discovered that this season was much busier than last, and that there were many backpackers like me, arriving in Ushuaia from all over the world, all hoping to get one of those last-minute passages. That if I had come the year before, the prices were half those of this year, and the number of last-minute berths far more plentiful. That this year, most ships were leaving with a full complement of passengers paying the full price. As was the case in the first two offices.

At the third office, the ships were also full. At the fourth, I was offered a cabin in a ship going out two days hence for $14,000; half the price it usually was, but still far too expensive for me. At the fifth, I was asked if I wanted to wait until mid-December, a period five weeks hence, then go out on a ship owned by a backpacker travel company known for their young clientele and hard partying. That one was being pitched as something that sounded more like a ten-day rave than a voyage out to ice that none of us were ever likely to see again.

I arrived at the sixth and final agency, feeling a mixture of pragmatism, despair and dogged hope. Tolkar Viajes y Turismo was fronted by a woman who had a gold plastic model of the Eiffel Tower on her desk.

'Have you been to Paris?' I asked, struck by the reminder of a Europe that seemed very far away right then.

Carla was from Buenos Aires. 'I spent two years working in France,' she said, and then, on catching my accent, 'I have an Irish friend from Galway.'

On that South American trip, I was travelling with two postcards of Ireland stuck in a flap at the back of my diary. I had them, not to allay homesickness – a state I've never once experienced – but as analogue images to show to people I met along the way. One postcard was of the Cliffs of Moher, in my home county of Clare, and the other was of Galway scenes; of Connemara bog and mountains and Galway city streets. I took out the Galway one, and showed it to Carla, who examined it with delight, as I assured her that her friend would know this landscape well.

Carla asked what she could do for me. I inhaled and sat down.

Tolkar represented a Chilean-registered ship called *Antarctic Dream*. As we were sitting in the office, it was cruising back towards Ushuaia, having almost completed its first expedition of the season. It was due to dock the next morning, and would depart again in the afternoon, and be gone for ten days. The passage out for its third expedition of the season in eleven days' time was already full.

'I suppose it's full for tomorrow too?' I asked.

Carla said yes. Then she checked her list again, and frowned. 'Let me call,' she said. The ship's home office was in Chile, in Santiago. She picked up the phone and there followed a conversation in rapid Spanish, with pauses. My Spanish was basic, and the conversation too swift for me to guess what was going on, but as I stared at the little gold Eiffel Tower, I was hopeful about the length of the call.

Carla put the phone down. 'There is one cabin left, going out tomorrow,' she said.

Yes! I thought. Yes!

Carla wasn't finished. 'But my colleague in Santiago has had someone else on the phone yesterday afternoon who is also here in Ushuaia and who is still thinking about it, a Danish woman. She is due to call back within an hour with her decision. So we have to wait.'

My first thought was: *I should have arrived a day earlier. I'm too late. Curses. Damnation. A pox on that other person. Get out of my cabin, Danish lady. Go far, far away.* 'How much is the cabin?' I managed to ask.

'That cabin is one of the cheapest, because it is very small, and just has a porthole. It's usually $12,000 for double occupancy, $10,000 for single occupancy. The last-minute price for tomorrow is $5,000. But it is presently being held by my colleague for the Danish woman.'

'Yes.'

'We will need to know the name of the person travelling by 2 p.m., because that is the deadline for registering the passenger list.'

'I will take that cabin if it is available,' I said, staring at the chart of Antarctica on the wall, a knot of tension forming somewhere in my innards.

'We must wait,' Carla said. 'My colleague will call back.'

I sat in that office for an hour or so, hardly breathing. I was afraid to leave and walk around outside in case someone else came in, also looking for a cabin; someone who might offer more for it. I felt almost dizzy. Everything took on a patina of unreality as I waited, suspended in time, my hands clutching each other with hope and longing, my head lost in images of ice and wandering albatrosses. The phone remained silent.

Eventually, Carla picked up the phone. 'I am going to call Santiago,' she said. 'Whoever is travelling, we need to get the passenger list completed.'

I watched Carla's face, wishing my Spanish was better. The conversation was short. She put the phone down, and smiled at me. 'The Danish woman has not called back.'

Five thousand dollars was more than I usually spent in months while on the road, but the destination was Antarctica, and I had saved up for the possibility of making this journey. There was a cabin! For the next day! 'Yes!' I said.

'Vamos Antarctica!' went the cry through the tannoy at 6 p.m. the following day, as the *Antarctic Dream* sounded its horn and pulled away from the End of the World, towards the Beginning of Everything. I was one giant atom of excitement, out on deck with the other passengers. Everything fell away as the gang-plank was pulled up: my latent fretting about the cost of the ticket; my regret that I was going to Antarctica alone, and thus would not be sharing this experience with someone I loved. All I could feel was a rush of pure joy, as the engines thrummed into action and the ship began to move south, towards the ice.

There were 43 crew and 70 passengers on the ship. These were some of my fellow passengers:

> A large group of Belgian family and friends, who numbered more than half the group and who occupied the two staterooms and most of the top-price cabins.

Two male friends from Ireland, both self-proclaimed millionaires, who told everyone they had made their money through property.

A dog groomer from Scotland. (The money in dog grooming, I found myself thinking, must be damn good.)

A trio of French bankers.

A group of Spanish friends.

A Swiss couple celebrating their wedding anniversary.

Various photographers on assignment for various magazines and sportswear companies, including *Vogue*, and The North Face.

Retired American businesspeople.

Four other 'last-minute' ticket-holder backpackers like me; two British couples. The five of us were by far the youngest passengers on board.

I went to sleep that night in Cabin 118, its porthole close to the surface of the water, which slapped methodically up against the glass. I felt like I was falling asleep in the ocean.

There were nature-themed talks twice a day on board before we reached the ice, and I learned how to recognize the birds that lived most of their lives on the wing: petrels, terns, fulmars, albatrosses. I had rented a down jacket and trousers in Ushuaia, and stood out on deck at intervals for as long as I could bear the bitter wind. The ocean was empty, but the sky was a thicket of wings, with the birds that followed the ship seemingly materializing from nowhere.

I saw my first wandering albatross with a surge of delight. From extended wing tip to wing tip, the albatrosses that glided past were longer than my body length. I could not stop watching them; mesmerized by their grace and power in the air. They were soon everywhere, these wandering albatrosses. When they were gliding, they balanced in the air on the tip of one long slender white wing, while the other extended far beyond their head; flexible airborne icicles.

The Christmas I turned fourteen, I received a camera from my parents as a gift. It came with two flash cubes; each one took four pictures. The flash cubes thrilled me. They looked like pieces of magical lucite, and their swift hard light as I pushed the button reminded me of the huge flash lamps that press photographers used in old black-and-white movies.

In fact, the plastic camera was the simplest and least fancy apparatus possible. I used up the entire roll of film and both flash cubes taking pictures of our Christmas dinner; of family members pulling faces, the decorated tree, and my mother's blazing pudding. It was months before I got the pictures developed, at the expense of a week's pocket money. They were terrible photographs: my family looked red-eyed and demented, and our Christmas tree was a watery green blob. I couldn't see the point of them. I'm not sure what I had expected, but it wasn't that. There was no thrill in returning to the past via those photographs. I never used that camera again.

We didn't take photographs in our family. It was never a thing, although my mother had briefly had a Box Brownie when I was a child. There were a few blurry pictures of summer holidays in Co. Kerry that she took, but nothing else. Unlike most families I knew, we did not ritually mark our rites-of-passage gatherings – birthdays, weddings, Christmas, holidays, anniversaries – with photographs.

By the time I was walking up the gangplank of the *Antarctic Dream*, I did not have a single picture of anywhere I'd been

or anything I'd seen. Antarctica was in fact the seventh continent I was visiting, but what I had come away from all of them
with were my diaries, various paper ephemera and memories,
not photographs. I wished I could sketch what I saw, as the
Victorians had done, but drawing was a skill far beyond me.

On the third day, the first ice appeared and drew us all out on
deck as one. From a distance, that first unforgettable iceberg
looked like the classic image of a sinking ship, its stern far
down, the bow at a distrustful angle.

'This iceberg has broken off from a glacier,' the guide
standing beside me explained. I was looking at the two groups
of flightless penguins standing in clusters at either end of the
iceberg, high up above the water. They were stranded there,
far above their food source, too far above the water to dive
down.

'The penguins will have to wait for the iceberg to melt,'
the guide explained, 'so they can slide or jump down into the
water. They're too high up at the moment.'

The iceberg was the height of a ten-storey apartment building. How fast could an iceberg possibly melt? I wondered. Our
ship passed by, the only thing moving in that landscape of
ice, apart from the gliding pelagic birds overhead. I borrowed
the guide's binoculars and trained them on the iceberg for
as long as it was in sight. The penguins looked the epitome
of stranded loneliness and isolation, hedging their collective
bets, huddled together at opposite ends of the iceberg, waiting
for their Godot.

After that first iceberg, the ice was everywhere. The
landscape became one of shifting, refracted light, with
an ever-changing architecture of ice. We passed roaming

icebergs the size of oil tankers, cathedrals, mountains. Ancient ice is compressed and a colour of blue that has no equivalent anywhere else; a colour of such unearthly depth and beauty I could only gasp the first time I saw it. Some icebergs were marked with uneven lines of colour like seams of precious gems. One had so much compressed ice within it that the entire iceberg glowed so fiercely I would have believed it could hold that light in the night.

It was a pristine landscape, empty of everything that referenced human habitation: no buildings, no roads, no people; almost, in a way, dystopian. 'Unearthly' was the word I kept writing in my diary, along with 'pristine'. There was a kind of majestic brutality to the scale of these icebergs. I could not begin to imagine how shocked the early explorers had felt when they saw icebergs from the fragility of their wooden ships.

Once we reached the ice, we made twice-daily landings, going out in small rigid inflatable boats called Zodiacs. We were divided into three groups named after Antarctic explorers: Scott, Ross, Cook. My group was Ross, after the British man who discovered Antarctica's Ross Sea in 1841. Our first landing was at a penguin rookery, where Adélie, Gentoo and Chinstrap penguins hardly stopped their stone-nest building to look at us. In a landscape of ice, stones are precious commodities, and I watched for hours as one penguin carefully deposited a stone on the snow, and another stole it while the first one returned to the water's edge for another.

In the blinding snow, the penguins slid and slipped and swam in all their comedic charm, utterly unfazed by our presence. There were huge brown skuas too, that prey on nests to steal the chicks. They sat on the snow like baskets of malevolence, waiting and watching. The seals slid in and out of the water. My boots sank into the snow, one after the other, as I walked around the rookery. *I am standing on Antarctic ground*, I thought, and shook my head in joyous disbelief.

It seems fantastical in an era of cameras embedded in phones and tablets, of Facebook and Instagram and Twitter, where images of people are so widely and constantly shared, that I have no idea what two of my grandparents looked like. In fact, before I ever travelled to Antarctica, I had a much better idea of what a place 16,000 kilometres from my home in Ireland looked like than the long-dead faces of my own flesh and blood.

All four of my grandparents died long before I was born. In the case of my paternal grandfather, he had died a fortnight before my father was even born; died aged thirty-six, of pneumonia. In my father's study, high up on a bookshelf, there were two studio photographs of my paternal grandparents, Patrick and Katherine. It wasn't until I was about ten that I was brought to visit my grandparents' graves: my mother's parents in a little vividly green cemetery in Glenamaddy in Co. Galway, and my father's in Lislaughtin, Co. Kerry, among the remains of a ruined abbey.

The only photograph I ever recall seeing of my maternal grandfather, Luke, was a tiny, blurred monochrome image of his face. My mother kept it in a flat round gold locket she sometimes wore, and I often went to her dressing table and opened the locket as a child to look at his minuscule, mysterious face. He was wearing a hat, but although I have often since tried to mine my memory, I remember nothing about what he looked like.

I do not recall ever seeing a single photograph of my grandmother Helen. My mother's parents were farmers in rural north Co. Galway. In a house where, like so many others in the townland, there was no running water, no car and no phone, there was no camera either. Luke and Helen both died the year my mother turned twenty-six; the year she met my father. The gold locket vanished along with almost all the rest of my mother's jewellery in a house theft when I was twenty-three, and along with it, my grandfather Luke's face.

On board the *Antarctic Dream*, it had soon become apparent that I was the only passenger without a camera. It was 2007, and the first iPhone had just been released that summer. The idea of taking pictures on your phone had not yet become routine, and I wasn't travelling with a mobile phone of any kind on that trip. At any rate, it was stand-alone camera hardware that my fellow passengers had; small point-and-shoot cameras, big Canons, Nikons, Pentaxes, and multiple lenses for each of them.

More than anywhere else I had ever been, it was Antarctica with its stark, unearthly beauty that had people constantly reaching for their cameras with an almost unnerving dedication. For the first time in years, I wondered if I had made a mistake in not bringing a camera along; if I was going to regret in the future this choice to forgo images from the white continent.

One evening, I sat beside Carlos, a Spanish passenger, who was digitally editing the pictures he had taken that day; all 1,000-plus of them. Beyond the windows, the icebergs, the albatrosses, the stunning, complex variations of icy whiteness.

Carlos swung his laptop round to face me. 'Look.'

I looked. There was a series of beautiful images of Adélie penguins in one of the rookeries we'd visited that day; another of the ever-changing mosaic of floating ice and icebergs. He had a great eye, and the technical skill to match. 'They're wonderful,' I said.

'You can never write about this,' Carlos said decisively, indicating my diary, which lay open before me. 'Nothing but photographs can capture this.' He waved an arm to the window and the Antarctic landscape beyond. 'All this.' He looked at me. 'Tell me. Do you honestly not regret not bringing a camera with you?'

I thought about it. My default reply to that question over the years had always been 'No', with varying accompanying reasons, along these lines. I did not like the distraction. I wanted to live in the moment. I preferred writing about my travels in my diary. I didn't like travelling with anything valuable. I didn't actually want any pictures. Why take bad pictures when I could get books with wonderful pictures of the same places? I didn't want to start stressing about 'capturing' things or 'missing' shots like a Victorian collector or hunter after their butterflies and big game. In truth, I had been not taking pictures for so long I had stopped thinking about it.

'I guess I'll only know the answer to that in the future,' I eventually said. 'But I haven't regretted it so far.'

Carlos just laughed, shook his head, and went back to editing his photographs.

I had never known my grandparents, but I did have an aunt and uncle I cherished. My aunt Máine and Uncle Gerry – always Uncle G to us – did not have children. They came and stayed with us for Christmas, during the summer, and at

Easter. In my childhood I spent a lot of time with them, and lived with them in Dublin my first year in college. All the love that would have gone into grandparents found its way to these two people instead.

My artist uncle was a marvellous cook, and coaxed me to try his home-made soused herrings, watercress salads, stews made from the mysterious beans he was always soaking. Once, when my parents were abroad, and I was about eight and staying in Dublin, I came down with measles. I awoke from a fever to find my aunt gone to work and my uncle sitting with me, reading the *Arabian Nights* aloud in his lovely, expressive voice. In my fevered state, the world Scheherazade incanted, of palaces and jinn and sherbet, took on a surreal quality. At that point in my life, I had never left Ireland. It was the first time I ever felt transported to another world, to a glorious faraway elsewhere.

My aunt, a linguist and supervisor of trainee teachers, did not cook. She filled the house with books, including the dishwasher, which I never once saw used for its original purpose. She did not drive, but knew the bus routes and timetables of central and suburban Dublin by heart, as she made her way from school to school to supervise and mentor the students she loved, fretted over, and whose careers she followed. She was so wedded to public transport that she was deep into her seventies before she reluctantly allowed me to hail her a taxi.

Three years before I went to Antarctica, my sister Cáitríona had called me at work one summer's day in a panic.

'Máine has just phoned me. The doctor has been, and says Uncle G might not last the day,' she said in a high, strained voice. My usually calm sister has an unusually rapid delivery of speech, sounding like someone on a speeded-up recording.

I'm used to it after a lifetime, but on that day, she spoke with such accelerated urgency that, for the first time in years, I had to ask her to repeat herself. The words had poured out like molten lava.

I had driven west that August afternoon at incoherent speed to rural Co. Galway, where Máine and Uncle G had moved after retirement. Uncle G, then ninety-six, died some twenty minutes after I got there, the three of us around his bed; myself, my sister and my aunt, holding his hands and his head. I had never seen anyone die before, and among the tears was a sense of awe that I was witnessing the end of a beloved life lived so long and well; 'a terrible beauty', as Yeats wrote in 'Easter, 1916'.

The following day, when the embalmers had brought him back, we laid him out on his bed for the wake. In the deep bedroom windowsill of the old cottage walls, I set about arranging an installation of bird books, paintbrushes, and their wedding picture; symbols of things that had meant so much to him in life.

'Loveen,' my aunt said, coming into the room as I was still trying to find the most pleasing composition of objects on the windowsill. 'Loveen, will you take some pictures for me?' She held out a disposable camera, and indicated the body of my dead uncle.

I looked at her with horror. 'Why do you want pictures of Uncle G when he's dead?'

'Please,' she said, then sat down on a chair and began again to weep. She could not explain to me why she wanted them; she just wanted me to do as she asked.

'OK,' I said eventually, taking the camera.

It had literally been decades since I had photographed the long-ago family Christmas dinner. I photographed my dead uncle with fastidious care. I stood on a chair and photographed his supine self, and then got down and crouched over him. I took images of details: the soles of his shoes, his face, his hands.

I realized as I was photographing him how much I had learned by osmosis from observing my press photographer colleagues over the years: get the overview, and then draw in tight; try to find the one image that tells the whole story. I thought it was his moustache, which he had had all his adult life, and still retained a smudge of in death. I took several pictures of his moustache. I used up the whole film, tenderly stroked Uncle G's alabaster forehead, and then gave the camera back to my aunt.

One of our landings was at a place called Port Lockroy, on Wiencke Island. The hut there was run by the British Antarctic Heritage Trust. It had first been a whaling station, and was then a British military base during World War II, although what purpose it served, being so far from Europe, I did not know. After the war, it operated as a research base. It was renovated a decade or so before we landed there, and Port Lockroy had the only commercial operation I saw in Antarctica.

Along with the stuffed penguins, the copies of *Lonely Planet Antarctica* and the branded fleeces, there were postcards for sale. It was a little ad hoc post office as well as a shop, and all the proceeds went to maintaining the site. We disembarked to get our passports stamped with a vanity visa that none of us, including me, could resist. The unnecessary stamp had the date, and the co-ordinates of the location. Port Lockroy, Antarctica. 64°49'S, 63°29'W. There was a little picture of a penguin with the words, ANTARCTIC HERITAGE TRUST, circling around it.

Four British people were working there, two men and two women, living there for the summer. They were collecting data on what effect the presence of cruise-ship tourists like us had on the penguins; half the island was a penguin reserve, although, of course, the penguins, unlike the tourists, were free to wander where they wished.

The hut was basic: two sets of bunks, a table, a few chairs, a crude kitchen, and not much else. It still contained some historical items from its days as a research station, after the war. The open shelving contained tins more than half a century old: Christmas pudding, stew, beans, peas, peaches. I lifted a tin of Christmas pudding, and realized with a surprise that it was full; still unopened.

'Sometimes they explode,' Maggie, one of the team members, told me.

'They explode?' I imagined Christmas pudding being propelled through the air; the long-confined raisins and candied peel and cherries breaking off like satellites.

'There's no heat or electricity in the hut, but it's because of the heat and humidity our bodies generate when we're here,' she said. 'Once or twice, they've just gone off like rockets. They had been left here for years, with no interruption to the humidity levels. They'll probably all explode eventually.'

The quartet had been at the base for three weeks, and ours was the first ship of the season that had called since their arrival. That night they came aboard the *Antarctic Dream* to shower and have dinner with us, and drink pisco sours. After three weeks of no running water, no electricity, and with only each other for company, they were unsurprisingly thrilled with the ship's luxury, the hot water, the conversation, the variety of food and the endless drinks. I sat with them, curious to discover more about how they dealt with the extraordinary isolation of their season's work.

'What do you do in the evenings?' I asked Maggie.

'We read the postcards,' she said.

Port Lockroy processes some 70,000 postcards a season, which means that the four people there have to share out the nightly task of franking the cards with the special Antarctic date stamps. To entertain themselves, as Maggie explained, they read the messages on the cards out loud.

I loved the thought of this gently voyeuristic way of passing long Antarctic nights: of finding out – when people were faced with the challenge of filling such a small white blank space – which words they choose to describe their unearthly surroundings. I loved the thought of the nightly readings of the inexhaustible trove of *Postcards from Antarctica*; a version of Scheherazade telling her endless stories in the *Arabian Nights* that Uncle G had told me all those years ago in childhood.

On the sixth day at sea, our Zodiacs set out to cruise through the seven-mile-long Lemaire Channel. We were to be the first passengers of the season to go through it. On the page that was slipped under my door each night, with the next day's programme on it, I had read that its nicknames were 'Fuji Funnel' and 'Kodak Canal', because the Lemaire Channel is so picturesque.

Each of the black Zodiacs held ten people. Ours was the last boat of the morning to load up and we were the last in a group of three Zodiacs; camera lenses bristling in all of them. As soon as we started to cruise the channel, I could see why it had got its nicknames. It was here that the ice was the oldest and most compressed of any I had seen so far. The icebergs glowed different shades of blue: turquoise, cerulean, azure, pavonated, sapphire, ultramarine. When our Zodiac stopped to allow people to take photographs I just stared at the surreal magnificence of that glittering blue ice. The other two Zodiacs had moved on and were now out of sight, as was the red-painted *Antarctic Dream*, hidden behind an iceberg.

'Vamos!' our boatman said, his hand on the tiller. But in the minute between stopping to take pictures and now, the pack ice had rearranged itself around the Zodiac. Our boat had, in the barest number of seconds we had stopped moving, become frozen into the ice: locked tight. The boatman rammed up the engine, but it made no difference. It was as if the white sky above us had broken and fallen into the sea in a billion shattered pieces of ice. He struck open the ice with an oar, revealing black water beneath. A second later, another piece of ice arrived like a furious magnet to replace it.

It took some time before we passengers realized we were stuck in the ice; our boat immovable as a beached whale.

'Why aren't we moving?'

'Is there something wrong with the engine?'

'Are we not meant to be following the other boats? Where are they?'

'I think we're stuck.'

'We're definitely stuck.'

'Man, it's getting cold out here.'

At intervals, there were frantic conversations in Spanish on the walkie-talkie our boatman had. Even in my thick down jacket, I felt the cold begin to slowly seep through, as we remained motionless in the ice. I remember the safety briefing we had got our first day at sea, when the crewman had functionally told us that anyone who fell into the Antarctic water would have less than three minutes to live before their body would go into shutdown.

An hour passed, and then another. One of the other Zodiacs attempted to reach us, but by now, the ice was spread out like a thick floor around us. My fellow passengers had long since stopped taking photographs and now, one by one, they stopped talking too. I kept staring at the blue ice, feeling as if I was in a strange dream. Coleridge's lines from *The Rime of the Ancient Mariner* came drifting back into my head.

> *And through the drifts the snowy clifts*
> *Did send a dismal sheen:*
> *Nor shapes of men nor beasts we ken—*
> *The ice was all between.*

> *The ice was here, the ice was there,*
> *The ice was all around . . .*

Our rubber boat gradually began to feel as fragile and vulnerable as the wooden ships of old. I wondered how long it would take jagged pieces of ice to start puncturing its compartments. It started to snow, and the white landscape got lost in the white snow. It was utterly silent. I looked at the ice floes; how much weight they could bear should our rubber boat slowly begin to deflate.

I thought about how Antarctica had become a repository of dreams for all those explorers; a place that nobody owns and that everyone can inhabit in their imagination. I thought of the penguins we had passed days before, stranded on an iceberg that might not melt fast enough for them to reach water and food, and wondered if they had reached water, and survival. I felt bewitched, looking at the blue ice, the cold seeping gradually through my entire body, thinking of Frank Hurley's famous photograph of the *Endurance*; its wooden structure clamped in the ice.

It took four hours for us to be rescued. The *Antarctic Dream*, unlike some Antarctic cruise ships, was not an icebreaker. It came towards us very slowly and cautiously: the crew could not afford to have it also disastrously stuck in the ice. The other passengers were all on deck, watching us through binoculars and waving encouragement. Crew members were standing holding blankets, and hot drinks, awaiting our recovery. When I saw one of the chefs in his white hat out on deck, taking photographs of us, I knew for definite that spending unexpected hours stuck in the ice was not a routine event.

The ship carefully nudged forward, little by little, until the bulk of its red starboard side was alongside our Zodiac. A ladder was let down, and one by one, we climbed up from where we were stranded in the frozen ice.

More than a decade has passed since I went to Antarctica. Now I have an iPhone, and thus a camera by default. The *Antarctic Dream* stopped cruising to Antarctica in 2012. My aunt Máine died in 2014, and I was with her when she died, too. After she died, my sister Cáitríona found the photographs I had taken of Uncle G among Máine's belongings in the nursing home, but I have never looked at them. Máine and Uncle G are gone into the same grave in Glenamaddy, Co. Galway, as my maternal grandparents, Luke and Helen, whose faces I don't have any photographs of.

I still don't regret not having pictures of what I saw in Antarctica, but what I have often thought about since is my conversation with Carlos. I keep wondering what he meant by all that was beyond the window, and told me only a camera could capture it. Perhaps his 'all this' was a pictorial record, but when I look back now at those ten days, my 'all this' comes down to the four hours stuck in the ice in the Lemaire Channel.

I can't remember who the other passengers were in the Zodiac that day with me, but I can recall the sensation of a life briefly lived in another dimension, a parallel world of unearthly beauty, in time out of time. I recall staring entranced at the blue ice; being colder than I had ever been before; and a thrilling feeling of dislocation and freedom, of being so far away from everything and everywhere. I recall thinking that some day I would die, and that from here on out, one of the rings in the bole of my life would be made of blue ice too hard to melt.

Peru
2008

ONISM

- awareness of how
little of the world
you'll experience

OMAR AND I were sitting in what had immediately become our favourite bar in Cusco, Fallen Angel. It was a glorious, kitschy place, with clouds painted on the ceiling, leopard-skin patterns on the armchairs, and tables which were antique baths that doubled as aquariums; a pane of glass on top, under which darted tiny, brightly coloured fish, swift as splinters of light. It was late in the evening, and we were slightly drunk. The rose-petal martinis were excellent, a thousand fairy lights were twinkling, and a mischievous-looking white angel with white wings was dangling precariously above our heads.

Omar was a Moroccan man I had met on a three-day trek into the Colca Canyon several days previously. There had been six of us who had signed up for the trek to climb down into the scenic canyons where condors fly. Two were an American couple who were very polite, but not much interested in talking to anyone other than themselves. Another two were long-time friends from California, and on the trek up and down the canyon paths, had frequently availed themselves of the mules.

Between the couple who were almost wholly focused on each other, and the mule-riding friends travelling at a distance above our range of hearing, Omar and I had spent many hours in step together, chattering away at length. He was on spring break from an MBA at an American university. Tall, lanky and full of energy, Omar was one of the smartest people I'd ever met, as well as being confident, funny and immensely likeable.

We had hung out together when we got back to Cusco: in fact, we were spending most of our time together during the day. Omar had persuaded me to go with him on another three-day expedition, this time into the Amazonian jungle east of Cusco, to a place called the Tambopata Reserve, near Lake Sandoval. We were due to leave in a couple of days, starting with a domestic flight from Cusco to Puerto Maldonado.

But for the last several minutes in Fallen Angel, we hadn't been talking about this forthcoming trip. In fact, I hadn't been talking at all. Omar had. He had recounted, in many articulate and flattering ways, how attractive he found me. How he hoped I felt something of the same attraction. How he hoped that we might now have a relationship that went beyond friendship.

'What do you think?' Omar said, stroking my hair, when he was done with his speech. He was smiling, while also regarding me carefully.

I did not know what I thought. I had remained silent while he was talking. I had not anticipated this declaration, and felt wholly unprepared for where the conversation might go next. It was true, though: as he had been speaking, I realized that there was indeed a now obvious chemistry between us; a mutual attraction that had been there almost right from the beginning. And yet. Omar was someone whose company I was thoroughly enjoying. He was handsome. He was extremely attentive. He was breathtakingly smart. And yet. And yet. What was stopping me?

'You're younger than me,' I said eventually.

'I know I am. So what?'

'You're much younger.'

Omar looked surprised when I told him my age, but unfazed. He shrugged his shoulders. 'It doesn't matter,' he said. 'Why would it matter?'

'It matters to me,' I said.

He stopped stroking my hair then and regarded me with puzzlement. 'Why?'

I looked him steadily in the eye. Omar knew why, surely. It simply wasn't the done thing for older women to have sexual relationships with younger men, even if they were going to be short-term. Something about it felt wrong to me. It wasn't wrong, of course. I was a product of a lifetime's Western conditioning about the role of women that society dictated. What was in fact wrong was this belief, almost watermarked into me, that I would be transgressing some societal norm should I actually respond as I wanted to Omar.

'It just does,' I said.

Men who had sex with younger women were studs. Women who had sex with younger men were cougars, predators, cradle-snatchers. Even the fact that there are so many more derogatory words in our vocabulary to describe women who have sex with younger men than the reverse illustrates an ingrained societal prejudice. But Omar was making it clear to me that he did not see it that way at all, and he had been brought up in a more restrictive culture than mine. He was honestly flummoxed that I would turn him down, not because the attraction wasn't mutual, but because of some set of rules in my head I felt I had to obey.

'Have I got this right?' Omar sounded baffled. 'Because I happen to be younger than you, nothing is going to happen?'

He wasn't trying to coerce me by talking like that. I did want to explore the possibility of something happening too; I was curious, and I was definitely attracted to him. But the mantra in my head kept screeching: he's twelve years younger! You hussy to even consider this! I looked up at the wings of the perpetually falling angel above us, suspended in his downward flight, and felt utterly confused. I'd never been in this situation before. My instincts and desires were battling it out with my social conditioning and the disapproving voices in my head. I was at the other side of the world from everyone who knew me. Nobody would ever know if I did in fact have sex with a younger man. But why would that even matter to me? What was really stopping me?

We sat there in silence for a while, leaning in against each other. I put my head on Omar's chest. His heart was beating wildly under my ear. He put an arm around my shoulders, and then tried to kiss me.

I sat up and pushed him away gently. 'I can't,' I said. 'I just can't.' I couldn't even look at him. I felt ashamed and conflicted and uncertain.

We sat apart from each other then, miserably regarding our forgotten drinks. 'But we can still be friends, right, Omar?' I said, almost choking on the awful clichés I was coming out with. 'I'll still go to Lake Sandoval with you.'

Omar didn't say anything for a while. Then he took both my hands in his. 'Why should it matter that there is an age difference?' he said evenly. 'You seem so independent and open-minded to me, but do you know how conservative you are underneath it all?' He wasn't angry as he delivered this statement; it was more that he seemed frustrated and, I realized with a lurch in my stomach, sad.

I was so taken aback by what I was hearing that I didn't know what to say. I had never once thought of myself as conservative. I had indeed considered myself independent and open-minded. I had not, in the main, lived a conservative life. And yet this person whom I had quickly grown to trust and admire and like was telling me that I was, in fact, innately conservative. Was he right?

Two days later, we arrived in Puerto Maldonado, after a forty-minute flight from Cusco. Cusco at once seemed like the most urban and knowingly savvy of places by contrast. It's the town where most tourists to Peru go; a lovely place anchored by stone and altitude, although it had seemed picked clean and packaged in some way to me, with little left to the imagination.

Here, close to the borders of both Brazil and Bolivia, it was evident at once we were in a different world; one dominated by the Amazonian jungle. It was humid and steamy, unlike the crisp, chill air of Cusco. Puerto Maldonado was a city once dominated by the rubber industry and, later, gold-mining. It is still defined by its busy ferry port, which is where we were taken to start our journey to the Lake Sandoval Lodge.

It had been raining heavily for the preceding two days, and Rio Madre de Dios was dark brown and swollen. The river was wide as a highway, and was, in fact, as busy as one. It was host to boats of all sizes. Our ferry boat was small and modest. We were going against the current, and as we started to move upriver, I soon realized that boats were not its only traffic.

Scores and scores of logged trees were travelling down-river at speed, their onward motion accelerated by their size and weight. The logged trees were on our left, and the boats navigated the right side of the river. But the recent rain had also brought random large branches down, and those branches were indiscriminate about where they landed in the water. Our boat was like a bumper car at the fairground; moving skittishly sideways and rocking hard every time an enormous branch thudded against it. It made me a little uneasy, but the boatman took no notice at all, apart from uttering intermittent strings of what I suspected were curses each time we were hit.

On either side of the river, the rainforest. The trees crowded the horizons beyond each riverbank. *Immersive* was the word that came to my mind. There was so much rainforest, it was almost bursting out of itself, like a snake shedding a verdant skin. The river was wide, but it was the rainforest that dominated the landscape.

Omar and I had agreed to remain friends but, of course, something had changed between us. You can't un-hear a declaration like the one he had made to me, nor can you un-hear the response to it. I was still privately mulling over his observation about what he perceived as my conservatism; by turns stung and offended, by turns doubtful and unhappy. I was unsure now if I had made the right decision, but as yet was barely able to admit that to myself. It was all irrelevant now anyway, I told myself. We would soon be separating for good, because Omar was due to return for his next semester, whereas I had months still to wander where I wished in South America. We sat beside each other now in the noisy boat, in companionable silence, watching out for the errant pieces of wood that were coming our way.

After an hour or so, we landed at a small dock; no more than a pontoon. We were the only two disembarking. Dante, our guide for the three days, was waiting for us there along with two porters, who took our modest rucksacks and some supplies that were offloaded from the boat.

Dante was composed of black curls, testosterone, and a kind of wild, dangerous energy that emanated from him almost physically, like sparks shooting from a downed electrical line. He had such presence; it was as if he fully occupied every cell of his being, and many more around him. He had none of the polite small talk most guides usually displayed on first meeting, with enquiries about your name, or where you were from.

'Put these on,' he instructed briskly by way of introduction, handing us each a pair of rubber boots. We did so. I had not previously paid much attention to the logistics of how we were to get to the lodge. It seemed that after the flight from Cusco and the hour-plus long ferry ride, we were still some distance away – a five-kilometre hike and another boat ride's distance away, to be precise. Before we started the hike, Dante gave us a short lecture, in bullet-point-type sentences:

'The rainforest is not a zoo: these are wild birds and creatures.

'Do not leave the path.

'For your own safety, you must obey what I say.'

Then he set off in front of us, at a fast pace, Omar and I following, with the porters taking up the rear. I soon learned that everything consumed in the lodge had to be carried in on this route, as there were no roads: this narrow muddy trail was the main way in and out.

Due to the recent rain, the path was awash with deep mud that was both slippery and sticky as wet clay. Along with the boots, we had been given a stick each. The purpose of the stick was not as a walking aid, but as a depth-sounder for the mud we were wading carefully through. As we went deeper and deeper into the jungle, the animals, birds and insects made themselves more and more evident. There were troupes of howler monkeys, blue and yellow macaws, morpho butterflies, their iridescent blue wings the size of two handspans.

'It's not a zoo, remember,' Omar joked, as we stopped to watch the parrots in a tree above us.

In places, we had to wade through ponds of muddy water that came almost to the top of our calf-high boots. My feet are a women's size four, and the boots I'd been given were far too big. I had to concentrate hard when fording these ponds, so that I wouldn't leave a boot behind in the mud. I had just forded the third or fourth of them when the porter behind me let out a yell. Startled, I looked behind me.

On the surface of the water I had just walked through was a white caiman, the smallest of the alligator family. Caimans may be the smallest in size, but their jaws and teeth are just as intimidating as those of their larger relatives. This one was snapping madly at the porter, who had almost stepped on him when the caiman was submerged. Caimans – I quickly learned – by and large are not dangerous to humans. But I did not know that right then. All I could see were those serrated rows of teeth which had been so close to my legs, just seconds before.

At the end of the hike, we were still not at our destination. Lake Sandoval is a large oxbow lake, and we had come off the trail on its western shore. The lodge was on the eastern shore. It was another half-hour by punt across the lake, and by the time we arrived at the little dock, I felt very, very far away from everything familiar.

Omar held out a hand to help me disembark. 'Happy you came?' he asked.

I was. It wasn't the kind of place I'd usually go to alone, but I wasn't going to be alone here; I had company. 'Yes,' I said.

Located on the shores of the lake, the little eco resort of Sandoval Lodge was not a fancy place. There were a number of thatched huts on stilts scattered throughout the complex. One was the simple bar and restaurant building. Accommodation was basic. The rooms had mosquito nets over the beds, a spartan bathroom, a large gap under the external door and, in my room at least, a general feeling that the wider world of nature was not very far away at all from its fragile walls and palm-thatched ceiling, pocked with holes.

There had been an awkward moment when Omar and I were being shown our rooms. Dante held the door of the first room open. I stepped inside. He remained standing there, holding the door open, looking at Omar.

'We're not together,' I said. 'We need two rooms.'

'Two rooms,' Omar repeated.

It was rainy season, and we turned out to be the only guests at the lodge. Dante explained that he would be joining us for meals, so we could ask him questions. In the dining room, I was struck by the absurdity of the pale pink tablecloths on each square table. They seemed so out of place there; so old-fashioned and somehow prudish, compared to the frantic wilderness outside. The complex worked on a generator that went off at 10 p.m., so we were warned to be in bed before then. The electricity didn't appear to have been connected to the fridge: our beers were warm. The knowing, kitsch sophistication of Fallen Angel and its rose-petal martinis in Cusco seemed, literally, to exist in another world.

'What do you want to ask me?' Dante said, when we were all sitting down together.

'Tell us about yourself,' I said.

There followed, in bits and pieces that night, a narrative more fantastical and compelling than I had ever heard from another human being.

He had grown up in this jungle, learning all its secrets and everything about the wildlife that lived there. By the age of ten, he was experimenting with a snake as a tourniquet on his arm. It worked so well, he needed the assistance of two grown men to get the snake off him again. At twelve, he was working in the Brazil nut industry. At thirteen, he was helping to log mahogany – the trees we had seen travelling downriver earlier that day. At fourteen, he was working in the gold mines.

Once he reached fifteen, he worked for a few years as part of a unit that trekked up to fifteen hours a day in the jungle, looking for drug cartels run by Colombians. He told us how their unit had found one cell deep in the jungle, five men and two women. How – or so Dante said – he had had to watch the main henchman being tortured, as first his fingernails were removed, and then most of his teeth. How that same man was then shot in the head. There were other stories about the fate of the two women; so gruesome I can't bear to repeat them.

By nineteen, he had moved to Lima. He met an English girl, and moved in with her specifically so he could use the opportunity to perfect his English. 'She was from Cambridge, England,' he recounted proudly, as if the English spoken in Cambridge was of a higher quality than anywhere else in Britain, except possibly Oxford.

At twenty-three, he came back to Lake Sandoval and began to work as a guide. He got married, and built the house he and his wife now lived in. He was in the process of building his own eco lodge; he planned to be running two of them by the time he turned thirty. 'Many Peruvians want to leave to go to America to earn money,' he said, 'but I think there is so much money to be made here in Peru, in eco lodges like this one.' He was currently studying Mandarin, as he figured that the Chinese were the next big untapped international tourism market. Suddenly he switched from English to Mandarin, speaking at speed. It was clear he was far advanced in his study of the language.

When Dante discovered that Omar was attending a prestigious business school, he quizzed him non-stop about what he had learned about entrepreneurship. Then, reluctantly, he left our table, telling us he would see us later on for the night walk.

Omar and I looked at each other that first night, both utterly agog, our warm beers forgotten.

'Do you believe all those stories?' he said. 'Or any of them?'

As a reporter, the need for facts, for evidence, for proof of assertion – of any story, let alone one as wildly outrageous as what Dante had just told us – is utterly innate. Of course, I had no way of knowing if he was in fact telling the truth. Yet I had found him a wholly plausible narrator. He had spoken with such articulate conviction, and in such detail, particularly about the discovery of the narcotics cell concealed within the jungle. 'I think so,' I said. 'Yes, I do.'

'Dante doesn't need an MBA from anywhere,' Omar declared. 'He is a born entrepreneur already. We should all be learning from him.'

It was dark by the time we had finished eating, but not late. We were to be there for two nights, and there was an activity planned for each of them. This evening, it was a night walk, and the following night we were due to go out on the lake. I went back to my room to fetch my head-torch.

When I opened the door and turned on the light, lizards ran at speed up the walls. I was used to having lizards and geckos in my room. I liked them. But as these lizards ran up the walls and vanished into the thatch, I found myself wondering uneasily about what else might be in my room. Despite the generator, the light from the single bare bulb was dim. The bathroom was partly open to the outside, as it had large gaps in the brickwork for ventilation. I went in there to brush my teeth, and soon decided to turn the bathroom light off, as huge moths with red eyes started to fly in through these openings.

Dante had already told us that, until recently, there had been an anaconda in the locality; an anaconda that had stolen and eaten an infant by swallowing her whole. That anaconda had been hunted down and killed. While acknowledging the tragedy of the child that was taken, Dante was indignant at the snake's destruction. 'This was its home. It belonged here.'

I had never heard of anacondas before and, that evening at the Sandoval Lodge, began to wish I had continued in my unwitting ignorance. Anacondas are one of the biggest and heaviest snakes in the world, equally at home in water and on land. They can grow to nine metres long, and weigh up to 227 kilos. They are not poisonous. At that size, they don't need to be. They are already a lethal squeezing machine. They wrap themselves around large prey – caimans, jaguars, humans if they can find any – and kill by literally squeezing the breath out of them.

I had anacondas in my head when I went out to join Omar and Dante. It was the blackest of nights in the belly of the jungle, so very far from any other settlements. The nocturnal jungle felt increasingly oppressive to me, as if it was slowly closing in on us; a great green predator itself.

'We start!' Dante said. He was armed with a stick, and a military-type torch, that cut blade-like precisely through the darkness.

'All set?' Omar asked.

I was not usually jumpy, but something about this jungle was making me incredibly jittery. Along with the stories of logging and gold-mining and searching for narcotic cells and anacondas, Dante had also told us about the guerrillas who had recently been raiding lodges like ours at night-time.

'They take their boats down Rio Madre de Dios at night, and then ambush the lodges,' he had said. 'They have Kalashnikovs. They rob tourists at gunpoint in the middle of the night, and then they escape by boat.' The last nightly raid had been as recent as two months previously. 'But Sandoval Lodge is safe! We are far from the river. The guerrillas would have to hike in to reach us here.' I had not been exactly reassured by this. I did not think I would ever recover my desire for travelling, should I wake up in the middle of the night, in the middle of nowhere, to see the ferocious barrel of a gun pointed at me.

'All set!' I said cheerily, adjusting my little head-torch.

Dante took the lead, and Omar walked behind me. Within minutes, we had seen three tarantulas. The first was on the path we were walking on, less than ten metres from the room I had just left, with its great big gaping gap under the door. The second and third, splayed out on tree trunks above our heads, resembled large hairy adult human hands with extra fingers.

'Look!' Dante cried happily. 'Tarantulas!'

I looked. I had had no idea what we were going to be seeing on our nocturnal walk, but I had definitely not expected
tarantulas, let alone three of them in quick succession. I don't
have a spider phobia, but really, tarantulas go beyond every
other kind of spider species. They are a species unto themselves. Their lore is bred into us. They're huge and they're
hirsute. They turn up in all kinds of movies, and they're not
usually there to be decorative.

'Wow,' Omar said. He was clearly curious to look at them
more closely. He shone his torch up into the tree, where one
of the tarantulas had stopped moving and was now staring
down at us. 'Isn't this amazing?' he said to me, excitedly.

I was not finding it amazing at all. I knew in theory it was
amazing – I was unlikely to see tarantulas in their natural
habitat ever again – but right then, what I was feeling was a
sensation of rising anxiety. All I could think of was my room,
in which I would soon have to spend the night alone, in the
dark, so permeable to the elements and the creatures of the
night and the possible guerrillas, and now on top of it all, these
bloody tarantulas.

We walked on a little further, and then Dante stopped to
poke at something with his stick. It was a small crevice at the
side of a bank. We watched as he continued to poke at the
hole. Then, things started to emerge from it, things that were
furiously waving small hairy legs. 'Baby tarantulas!' he cried
gleefully. He was trying to encourage them to take a grip on
his stick. An adult tarantula – the mother? the father? who
knew? – also angrily appeared out of the hole. Dante had managed to get one baby spider to climb on to his stick, and was,
I realized with horror, now in the process of carrying the stick
over to Omar and me.

'No, please stop,' I said, my voice a curious high-pitched tone. Instinctively I reached to clutch at Omar, and our hands snapped together as if magnetized. I was mortified. Mortified at being the clichéd female scared of spiders. Mortified at showing my fear to Omar and Dante. Mortified at the fact that I was now gripping Omar's hand so tightly.

'It's only a baby spider,' Dante said, moving ever closer to us. 'You're not scared of it, are you?' The tarantula was clinging fast to the stick that Dante was now thrusting in my direction.

Omar stepped out in front of me, blocking the stick, still holding my hand. 'The lady doesn't like this,' he announced sternly. For a second, I had a ridiculous image in my head of a protective Victorian hero: I could not think of the last time anyone had referred to me as a 'lady' in ordinary conversation.

Dante laughed and laughed. He thought it hilarious that I was frightened of something so much smaller than me. But he shook the stick, and the spider ran away into the shadows, back to its tarantula nest.

'We go on!' he announced.

We were still less than ten minutes at most into what was meant to be an hour-long walk. Adrenaline was pulsing through my body to the extent that I was almost shaking. Right then, I simply could not face the thought of discovering jumping spiders, or snakes, or nocturnal tree frogs, or all the other things Dante was now promising we would see. The jungle seemed suddenly like a kind of sinister three-dimensional lift-the-flap picture book. With every few steps we took, something hidden would literally pop up out of nowhere at us. I felt wholly unprepared for this night, in every way.

I tugged at Omar's arm. He leaned down at once. 'I'm so sorry, but I want to go back,' I said. 'But you go on.' At this point, I didn't care how much I was publicly humiliating myself. I just had to get away from the night jungle.

Omar straightened up again, and called to Dante. 'We are going to go back,' he said decisively.

Dante was astonished. 'We have only started!'

'We are going to go back,' Omar repeated, and started to walk back with me to the lodge.

We had returned to have another warm beer in the empty restaurant. Dante had come with us, then excused himself to visit the bathroom. When he rejoined us, he slapped his hairy hand down on the pink tablecloth.

'Do you know what I saw just now in the staff bathroom, Rosita?'

I looked at him with fury. He knew perfectly well that the staff block was next to my room.

'What? What did you just see, Dante?'

'A tarantula! I put it out the window. Maybe it will climb into your bathroom now!' Then he left us.

I had no idea if Dante was joking or not. Beside me, Omar was heroically trying his best not to laugh. I felt like crying. A kind of terror was beginning to spread through me. My imagination was violently afire. While absent from my room, my imagination had populated it with snakes, anacondas and tarantulas big and small. It now added guerrillas hiding in the jungle, waiting for the lodge to vanish into darkness at 10 p.m., when they would find their unerring way to my room.

'Your mistake was to show him your weakness,' Omar said. We were still holding hands. 'It's the same in business. Now he knows what it is, he is going to be ruthless, and keep going after it.'

Our roles had totally reversed from two nights previously. In Fallen Angel, I had been the one with the power, although I had not thought of it as such at the time. In the humid, mosquito-filled restaurant we were now in, I felt that all my usual confidence had seeped away, leaving me an utter neurotic wreck at the thought of the night ahead.

When it was approaching 9.45, we both got up. Unless we wanted to fumble our way to bed in the dark, we needed to avail of the last minutes of the generator.

Omar stopped at my door; he waited for me to open it and switch on the light. 'Goodnight,' he said then, and gave me a hug.

'Goodnight,' I said, hugging him back, and then closed the door before he could see in my face how scared I was at the prospect of sleeping alone.

I had gone to the loo back in the restaurant, and did not go into my bathroom now. I didn't care that my teeth were unbrushed, or my face unwashed. I shut the bathroom door as firmly as I could, but the wood had long since buckled in the humidity and it did not quite close. The light from the generator went out suddenly, but not before I had again been reminded of the large gap under the door that led outside.

I crawled in under the bed's mosquito net, fully clothed. If the guerrillas came to get me in the night, at least I wouldn't be buck naked when they arrived. I lay rigid beneath the mosquito net, my head playing and replaying footage of the tarantulas in my head. Omar was in the next room, but he might as well have been back in Cusco, he seemed so far away right then.

Lying sleepless in bed, I conducted an existentialist battle with myself. I now very badly wanted to be with Omar. It would be thrilling and romantic and fun to have sex in such a febrile place. Also, crucially, I would no longer be sleeping alone: the two of us would fall asleep eventually, tightly entwined into each other. My night terrors would vanish. I might even be able to joke about tarantula squatters in our bathroom. Yet I continued to lie there, in my own bed, in my own room, alone.

But did I want to be with Omar now just because I was scared, or was it because I genuinely found him attractive? Was it OK to change my mind? Was it cheating, giving in, to be with someone so they could act as a convenient buffer between you and your fears? But cheating whom? Giving in to whom, or what? What the hell did it even matter? Why was I voluntarily depriving myself of an extraordinary experience?

I was still smarting from the description of my character as conservative, and a large part of me was traversing in my head that invisible border. I was now wondering what, in fact, would it be like to actually have sex with this man I had grown to like so much in the last several days. It would be so easy to leave my room and knock on Omar's door. I had total confidence that I'd be welcomed in.

In the end, stupid stupid stupid, useless pride kept me tethered to my bed.

'Sleep well?' Dante enquired at breakfast next morning, grinning across at me.

'Yes,' I lied. I had had vivid nightmares and, as a result, had woken several times, convinced that there was something either critter or human staring at me in the darkness. I had jumped out of bed as soon as the pale grey dawn arrived, and taken my diary to the dining room to write, where the walls seemed a lot more solid than those in my room. On my way there, I had gone down to the pontoon landing on the lakeside, and looked across the enormous lake. It was drizzling lightly and a mist was suspended over the water like a levitating, undulating ghost. I looked across the surface of the slate-coloured lake and wondered what it contained that I could not see; and what the persistently green jungle that surrounded it contained.

I was braver in the daylight. I could see what was coming at me. We went out in the boat early that morning, to see the giant otters swimming. They were freakish-looking, as if they were the product of some weird genetic lab experiment, because they were on a wholly disconcerting scale to the otters I knew. These giant otters were feeding on piranha fish. We could see the food chain in action right in front of us. Everything was literally trying to eat something else.

'Don't fall in!' Dante joked, poking me with an oar. Omar had been right. Once Dante knew how jumpy I was around the more unusual wildlife, the more ruthlessly he tormented me. The only piranha fish I knew of were the ferocious ones that would take your flesh off in seconds should you be so unlucky as to fall into water where they swarmed in shoals.

When he was not being an asshole, Dante was a formidable guide. His knowledge of the jungle was comprehensive, and he could read the landscape so closely. Where we saw nothing but trees that looked the same as all the other trees, Dante spied sloths hanging upside down, and took us over until our boat rocked quietly beneath them. The primeval-looking sloths, high in the trees, did not budge as we regarded them.

There were small turtles basking on logs, and more giant otters. Sandoval felt less oppressive to me out on the open water. Being on the lake was certainly the most startling show-case for the birdlife.

'Look!' Dante called. A pair of toucans flew past us. Toucans!

Then red-bellied macaws.

Blue and yellow macaws.

He took us in again under some trees, and pointed upwards. Above us, drilling precisely, was a woodpecker, the sound it was making constant as the ticking of a metronome.

There were weaver birds, ospreys, kingfishers, and birds that darted past us so quickly, they were gone in a glorious blur of scarlet or peacock-blue or jade.

Later in the day we went on a long walk, deep into the jungle, to where the Brazil nut trees grew. Omar took a firm hold of my hand as soon as we set out, and I was glad.

I had never given a Brazil nut any thought in my life, other than noting that they were both expensive and delicious. We walked towards the interior of the jungle for a good hour, then were suddenly among a stand of old Brazil nut trees. Most nuts that make it out into the Western world come from pristine forests like these: the trees can't be grown commercially as they require such levels of natural pollination. There were, of course, no roads in the jungle, just trails, one of which we were on. Before we had even reached the trees, we had realized that the harvest would have to be carried out. It struck me I had not seen a single mule since we had arrived: this humidity was not an environment they would thrive in.

We never knew what Dante was going to surprise us with next. This time, it was a machete. It was January, the rainy season, when we were at Lake Sandoval, and the nut harvest was under way. Local people have the right to harvest the nuts, and to make their living from them. They had been there the day before and would soon be returning.

'Keep back,' Dante instructed, making us stand beyond the perimeter of the trees. He pointed upwards and we saw, far above our heads, objects that looked like coconuts, except rounder, the same shape as footballs. These were the pods in which the nuts grew. Once the rainy season began, they started falling to the ground. We could see why Dante was keeping us away from the spread and reach of the trees: if you were hit on the head by one of those pods, you were a goner. As we stood there, I meditated briefly on my possible obituary: *She died when struck by a falling pod of Brazil nuts in the Amazonian jungle in Peru.* It was a good opening line, but not one I wanted to come true.

Dante walked around the base of the trees, searching for a pod that had already fallen. He found one, and came back with it. It was very heavy, and sealed tight within its own shell.

'The pods have to be opened here,' he explained. 'It is easier for a man to carry the Brazil nuts out of the jungle than it is for him to carry the whole pod.' It sounded almost biblical, the way he said it. I was beginning to understand why the nuts were so expensive, but I had never realized they were so storied.

Dante invited us each to try opening the pod with the machete. I whacked it with all my strength. The blade bounced back from the shell like a gun recoiling. Omar tried. He made some progress, creating a deep slit in the surface. Dante, of course, split the pod with a single effortless-looking gesture. He had been doing this since he was twelve, he reminded us. I stored that away in my head as evidence of the probable truth of the rest of his wild stories.

There were about twenty nuts in the pod, which we dug out. It's in this form that they are carried out of the jungle, on the backs of men and women, before they are sent across the world in planes or ships, to end up in our kitchen cupboards. The three of us ate some of the nuts right there, standing near the tree from which their pod had fallen. I felt suddenly inarticulate with humility to have learned the origin story of the Brazil nut. There was so much we did not know about the world, and never would, no matter how far we travelled and how much we saw or experienced of it.

That night we went out on the lake in a kayak. Dante took one paddle and Omar the other. I was to be the lookout, using Dante's powerful torch. It had been raining, and the clouds obscured any starlight. It was a thick, deep, noisy darkness, out there on Lake Sandoval at night.

'Tonight we will see many black caimans,' Dante said. 'Rosita will find them for us!'

The two of them paddled across the lake to the western shore, pulling together in an easy rhythm. I sat in the boat, dreaming, while the paddles plashed in the water. A tiny scrape of a new moon edged into view between the clouds. I wondered if anacondas were moving somewhere in the vast lake, far beneath the hull of our canoe, undulating in their extraordinary length like flexible aquatic trees. I wondered had the local people gone after the anaconda who had taken the baby with the demented rage of Ahab after Moby Dick? Of course, one narrative was true and the other was fiction, but they both seemed utterly fictional to me on the surface of it: a feared reptile of terrifying size and power stealing away a human life, and the largest mammal in the world being hunted down by an enraged man who wanted revenge for his lost leg, and the destruction of what he described as the 'intangible malignity' of Moby Dick.

We stopped close to the shoreline. 'Now,' Dante said. I had been instructed to rake the undergrowth closest to the shore slowly with the torch, and not to let the beam remain too long on any one spot, as that would attract large and eager bats. I switched on the torch and began to move the beam slowly along the area where the water flooded in against the trees.

'There,' I said. I had found my first black caiman. The black caimans were a far larger version of the white caiman the porter had come so close to stepping on during the hike the other night. They looked exactly like alligators. The light had caught the curious orange of the caiman's unblinking eyes, not a metre away.

I proved to be excellent at locating caimans. We were out for an hour, circumnavigating the lake, and I found probably thirty caimans. The odd time, they sank beneath the water when the boat came close, but mostly they stared back at us with those eerie sodium-orange eyes, their medieval-looking knobbly backs breaking the surface of the water. It was absurdly thrilling, but the thought of an imminent turning in for the night was beginning to consume me uneasily again.

We were due to leave early the next morning. For the second time, Omar walked me to my door shortly before 10 p.m., and waited while I opened it and turned on the dim light. 'Good-night,' he said, hugging me.

I hugged him back, unable to say anything. Was it all too late now for anything else between us? Why had I wasted so much time wondering what was the right thing to do? But what *was* the right thing to do? It wasn't just the age difference. It was the fact that we were not equals in our life experience. But who was I, to be some kind of judge over what kind of life someone needed to have lived before they were allowed to cross some invisible border?

'You all right?' Omar asked, still holding me tight.

'Yes,' I said.

Iceland
2015

ENFILADE

- a number of things
arranged as if strung
on a thread

THE FIRST TIME I ever heard the word Iceland was when I was about nine. Iceland. I thought it was a storybook name for a country. I had loved the fairy tales of the Brothers Grimm and of Hans Christian Andersen. The ice in Hans Christian Andersen's Snow Queen story had stayed with me. Ice that could penetrate hearts and eyes; a frozen lake composed of a puzzle of ice that Kai could not solve; the puzzle that the Snow Queen had called the Mirror of Understanding. I had not understood what it meant; all I knew was that it had troubled me in some way I could not articulate when I had read it.

> Kai was dragging along some pointed flat pieces of ice, which he laid together in all possible ways, for he wanted to make something with them, just as we have little flat pieces of wood to make geometrical figures with, called the Chinese Puzzle. Kai made all sorts of figures, the most complicated, for it was an ice-puzzle for the understanding. He found whole figures which represented a written word, but he never could manage to make just the word he wanted. That word was 'Eternity'.

In 2015, one of my editors came to me with the offer of a press trip. An Icelandic airline was to start the first direct flights from Dublin to Reykjavik later that summer. Would I go there in advance of the direct flights? It was not to be a press trip per se, where you were escorted around with other journalists on a planned visit. It would just be me, making my own itinerary for three nights. I would be flying via London. My flight and hotel would be paid for by the airline and a local tourist company, as would a visit to the Blue Lagoon, and whatever day trip I wished to take out of Reykjavik.

'Would you like to go?' she asked.

I did not take long to answer.

'There are many wonders in a cow's head,' read one of the billboards at Keflavik Airport; a non sequitur accompanied by a huge image of a bovine head. *What?* I couldn't stop laughing at the randomness of this welcome. The journey via London had taken twelve hours so far, since I'd left home that morning. I had fallen asleep once we had departed London, and awoken to look down from the plane on to empty, snowy tundra, broken only by the distinctive collapsed cones of volcanoes and glittering lakes. I could not believe this place would soon be only two hours by air from Dublin: it felt so much further away already.

On the short bus journey from the airport to the Blue Lagoon, the lack of sleep due to my very early start had initially made me feel foggy. But the landscape I was looking at now jolted me to sharp consciousness. The clarity of the light was astonishing: everything in such intense focus that my eyesight felt preternaturally improved, as if I could suddenly see for miles.

The dream-like element of arrival to the country continued as I slipped into the steaming, powder-blue water. The lagoon was not very deep, but I managed to swim to a quiet section, then stood up like a geothermal centaur; half my body perished with the insistent wind, half held in a beguiling, seductive, blue warmth. Skeins of geese flew overhead like avian calligraphy across the moss-covered lava fields – an image right out of one of my childhood books of fairy tales.

Once upon a time, I had been engaged to be married. I had first met Lewis, an Englishman, in Kathmandu, where our separate journeys in Nepal crossed by three days. I had met him again a year or so later, when I was briefly back in England, and then some time after that, we had become engaged.

In a jeweller's in the glass-covered arcade of the Victoria Quarter in Leeds, I had chosen a ring, its row of little diamonds glimmering like a beautiful, hopeful line of light. After we had got engaged, we lived together in Yorkshire. Lewis took me one day to Heptonstall in Yorkshire's West Riding, to see Sylvia Plath's grave. It was winter, and we shivered as we wandered around the graveyard, looking for the grave of the dead poet.

At one point when I lived in London, I had gone to look for the house in Primrose Hill where Plath had lived and died. A poet herself, she had recorded with delight in her diary that the house at 23 Fitzroy Road had a blue plaque to commemorate the fact that W. B. Yeats had lived there between the ages of two and eight. It was here she had come to live with her two children after her marriage ended; where she had written her Ariel poems; where she had died by suicide. I had found the house, and been disconcerted to discover that the exterior bore no evidence of her presence. There was only the blue plaque to Yeats. I stood quietly outside the house for a while, imagining her coming in and out the front door, the lines of brilliant unwritten poems scrawled inside her troubled head.

Now Lewis and I stood beside her grave. *In Memory, Sylvia Plath Hughes 1932–1963. Even amidst fierce flames the golden lotus can be planted.* I had gathered some greenery from the winter hedgerows, and placed them on her grave. Afterwards, we had gone to one of the nearby pubs on a steep street, where we drank real ale and talked about the sadness of such a life ended far too soon.

It was about the time we went to Heptonstall that Lewis and I began to realize we were not, in fact, destined to get married to each other. It was around this time too, while trawling in a charity shop in Leeds, that I found a little handmade cardboard box. It had been fastened together with tiny metal staples and hinges. On the lid was a date written in black pen, 28–2–61, and the words, 'An Eastern Street Scene' and then in small, neat capitals, 'Complete, very testing little puzzle.'

Inside the box was a handmade jigsaw. The pieces were not like ordinary jigsaw pieces, where two or three shapes repeat for the whole puzzle. These were all exquisitely cut different shapes; each one a tiny work of art in itself, some no larger than a fingernail. I bought the box for a pound, and brought it home to the rented attic flat in Headingley where we were living.

'Look what I found,' I said to Lewis.

'Let's make it,' he said, shaking the pieces out on to the table.

'There are probably pieces missing,' I said.

'Bound to be. Made in 1961 and all.'

We leaned in together, sorting scraps of sky, and fruitlessly searching for anything that suggested edges. There was not a single conventional jigsaw piece in the whole puzzle. As we painstakingly started to put some pieces together, we realized that the maker had deliberately made the puzzle as complicated as possible, by carefully cutting along the outlines of objects. Nothing connected in any obvious way. We just had to keep trying to fit different pieces together, one after the other.

'This is bloody hard,' I said, when we had been at it for half an hour, with very little completed.

'But fun,' Lewis said, delighted we were not arguing or being silent with each other, as had become worryingly usual.

'But fun,' I agreed.

As we slowly pieced together the little puzzle, the image gradually revealed itself. It was indeed an Eastern street scene; a Middle Eastern street scene, with minarets and carpet-sellers and men in long robes, with wooden balconies overhead and windows open to the heat. We kept marvelling over the fiendish, creative genius of the person who had made the puzzle. I started to fret that there would be missing pieces. I very much wanted it to be perfect and complete.

Not only was every piece there, the creator of the puzzle had left a secret for whoever completed it. They had incorporated their initials into it. Lewis and I regarded our joint work with joy; laughing and happy, speculating on the person who had made this wonderful thing and wondering how such a treasure had ended up in a charity shop.

Lewis picked up the box again. 'Complete, very testing little puzzle.' He looked at me with a hope and optimism that I shared. 'Just like our relationship. Maybe we can figure it out and make sense of it together, like we did with this.'

What we soon figured out together about our relationship was that it was over.

I returned to Dublin a couple of months later. I was in my early thirties, and starting all over again. I had been away from Ireland on and off for years. I did not have a job, had lost touch with many of my old friends, and now no longer even had a relationship. I spent that summer working as a temp. I had one lovely job at the beginning and then a succession of unlovely ones. Throughout that summer, I applied for jobs in the arts sector; I did not receive a single reply, let alone an invitation to an interview. Meanwhile, I typed letters, took inarticulate dictation, answered phones and realized with dismay that my default name between the hours of 9 a.m. and 5 p.m. was now 'You', or sometimes, 'Hey, You.'

As the summer progressed, I wrote to some newspapers, offering articles about Iran or Pakistan, where I had travelled a few years previously. Occasionally, while elsewhere, I had handwritten such pieces about the places where I was, and posted them to the *Irish Times*, which, astonishingly, had published them all. The last piece I had had in the paper was about Varanasi, in India.

My letter to the *Irish Times* arrived the week when India was to mark the 50th anniversary of its independence. Someone remembered the previous piece I had written about Varanasi. An editor called me, and asked if I could file – I had to ask him what 'file' meant – 2,000 words on my experiences in India for two days hence. I agreed without knowing whether I could or not, called in sick to my temping job the following day, dug out my travel diary from that period, and duly hand-delivered the one and only floppy disk I ever wrote anything on to the newspaper's offices. The piece was carried on the cover of the paper's Saturday Weekend supplement, and in my subsequent euphoria, I found myself wondering if perhaps I could write other articles too.

That week, from my temping job, I faxed – faxed! – three ideas for stories to the then features editor, Caroline Walsh.

She called and instructed me to do all of them; an act of faith in a totally untested writer I was determined to honour. When I had written the first piece, she asked me to come into the office with the printed copy, so that, as she put it, 'I can have a look at you.'

I went up to the fourth floor of the building we then occupied, and gave Caroline my article to look over. Later, I used to think of her as a restless bird; her busy, ever-stimulated mind was always flying in so many different directions at once, rarely settling in any one place for long. She herself was the daughter of a famous author, Mary Lavin, who wrote many short stories for the *New Yorker*: Caroline had long known the value of stories of all kinds.

Caroline read the article while simultaneously firing questions at me. What had I read at college? What had I been doing until now? Did I not know I should always, always, always ask someone's surname when interviewing them? (I was so clueless back then that I had not in fact known this most basic rule of interviewing.) Was I serious about journalism? Did I know I could write?

I answered as best I could, disconcerted to be addressing the side of her head, which was bowed over the printed pages that she was marking swiftly as she read. When she reached the end of the article she let out a whooping kind of laugh and said, 'Yes!' although whether that was meant for me or her, I did not know. It was a long time before I realized that Caroline having 'a look' at me that day was the closest thing I ever had to a formal job interview at the paper.

No more than a fortnight later, I had left my temping job and was actually sitting working at a desk in the features department of the *Irish Times*, being unofficially mentored by Caroline. At the start, I was a full-time freelance contributor, then I was offered a writing contract, and after that, a staff job. It would never happen like that today. Freelance contributors are not permitted to work in the building, and work from home these days, thus missing the opportunity to learn by osmosis on the newspaper floor. I am probably one of the last people working there now who came to the paper via a life-path other than an MA in journalism or a work placement. I learned everything I knew about journalism simply by being in the office and by doing the work, but most importantly, I learned from Caroline's initial direction.

I discovered that I loved to report, to interview, to write. I loved the buzz of a newspaper office; the fact that every assignment and every day was different; the unshakeable communal dedication to deadlines; the thrumming of the presses in our Fleet Street basement that started in the late afternoon; the exhilaration of picking up the newspaper and seeing my byline and story in print. I delighted in the fact that I could report on whatever subject was currently provoking my curiosity; marvelled at the privilege of being allowed into the lives of all sorts of people, to tell their stories; thrilled at the adrenaline rush of being on a developing story. After so long wandering the world and doing short-term jobs in between, I knew almost right away I had finally discovered my true career.

What overjoyed me most of all was the fact that it was my travels that had led me to journalism. I had not, in the end, been throwing away an opportunity for a career. The experiences I had had in so many different countries and cultures were in a way an apprenticeship for being a reporter. I had learned to be observant, and patient, and how to talk to all kinds of people and deal with all sorts of situations, and to be endlessly curious. And best of all, without the articles I had written and sent back from elsewhere, none of the rest of it would ever have happened, and I would not now be in Iceland, standing in the Blue Lagoon, on this ad hoc press trip.

Reykjavik had a sassy line in souvenirs. It was a few years since its unpronounceable volcano, Eyjafjallajökull, had erupted and caused all transatlantic flights to be cancelled for days. I had myself been affected; while I was in the air on my way to a reunion of friends in Dallas, Texas, the volcano had erupted, stranding me for several additional days in the US. I had revelled in telling anyone who would listen, 'I am stranded by volcanic ash'; a sensational line I did not think I would ever get the opportunity to use again. It was also some years on from the country's extraordinary economic implosion. One excitable popular slogan that appeared on many mugs, T-shirts and coasters managed to combine both recent events: 'Don't fuck with Iceland! We may not have cash, but we've got ash!'

Another popular T-shirt was one designed to look like a Facebook update. It read, 'I had sex with an elf in Iceland.' In the same shop there were boxes of condoms branded 'Iceland Eruption', with the description, 'high quality condoms from the land of explosions'. Perhaps the person who had just announced via Facebook that they had had sex with an elf had availed of them.

I was fascinated by the viscerality of some of the souvenirs and craftwork sold in the independently owned shops along the main shopping street, Laugavegur. There was a toy for children that looked as if it had come right out of the Addams Family toybox: something called Creative Fishbone Model

Making, made from actual 'sterilized fishbones'. There were candles called PyroPets; when the wax melted down, they revealed eerie metal skeletons of unidentifiable creatures with huge eye sockets.

The landscape and the natural world appeared to permeate everything. I lost count of the number of necklaces and pendants I saw made from bird bones, bird claws, and animal teeth; some dipped in silver, some in oxidized bronze. I coveted a pair of handmade fish-skin leather shoes that came in shades of deep pink and gold and peacock blue, like something a crazed princess in a fable would wear.

It all seemed to have been too much for one visitor: too many grungy cafés with mismatched and salvaged furniture; too many truly beautiful locals; too many beards and Nordic jumpers and handmade fish-skin shoes. 'Iceland is fucking pretentious' read the anguished graffiti in English I saw painted on a white wall somewhere along the main street of Laugavegur.

I soon learned that the Icelandic for puffin is 'lundi'. The lundi were everywhere. There was one the size of a small bear outside a tourist shop, children burying their faces in the white fur of its giant breast. Lundi came stuffed in all sizes and their images were on everything you could possibly imagine, including a pair of tights on display in one boutique; possibly the weirdest fashion accessory I have ever seen in my life. I tried, and failed, to imagine anyone I knew wearing those tights. The lundi also turned up smoked on the menu at the many Icelandic banquets advertised outside restaurants, along with whale and reindeer.

As I walked along Laugavegur, I could see the dark blue, white-flecked sea appearing and disappearing at the end of streets; dramatic slices of ocean. The wind was bitter and the air was utterly pure and clean. The sea commanded everything: it did not take me long to discover that Iceland means 'island'.

In my wandering, I turned a corner and found myself looking at an entire mosaic wall, the height and width of the building it was on: the city's Custom House. It was utterly extraordinary: a beautiful expanse of a scene that depicted, in abstract, a harbour and ships. I looked at it first from the opposite side of the street, marvelling at its size, intricacy and colours – gold, ochre, amethyst, burnt sienna, eau de Nil, saffron, primrose; and especially the many different shades of blue; azure, robin-egg blue, cobalt, cyan, Prussian blue, indigo.

I crossed the street and went right up to it, touching the mosaic, and walking alongside it. I realized that parts of the mosaic were composed of pieces of quartz and what looked like semi-precious stones. Midway down one part, at about my shoulder height, was an incredible piece of smoky quartz, cut to reveal its many gradations of colour, all the way from chestnut through cinnamon, amber, and finally, pure white. In the centre of this whiteness were five tiny pieces of gold. You had to look very carefully to see them, but there they were. I was looking at what appeared to be a jewelled wall.

I ended up that first day at Hallgrimskirkja, the improbably beautiful pale-coloured church that looks like a masterful installation of icicles, and is named after an Icelandic poet and clergyman. I could imagine the Snow Queen imperiously marching out of its front door, wearing a crown composed of shards of ice and trailing a long white cloak. The Expressionist architect, Guðjon Samúelsson, designed the church to reflect the glaciers and ice and mountains of Iceland. You can see it from wherever you are in Reykjavik, rising above the city's roofs like a slender iceberg. The bells rang out from above while I was circumnavigating its base, and I heard it as a kind of benediction.

Back in 2004, I had been on a press trip to the Faroe Islands; this one a formal trip, with several other journalists. The Faroes are an archipelago of eighteen tiny islands, seventeen of which are inhabited. Everything there was defined by the sea: the fishing economy, the traditions of whaling, the ferry crossing from one tiny island to another.

I had been fascinated by the way the sea had even made its way into the archipelago's Lutheran churches. We were told that the area where the congregation sat was called the ship, because in the Faroes, you sail through life. In one church, in Klaksvik, an actual fishing boat hung from the rafters. In another – a tiny whitewashed one overhanging the ocean at Kirkjubøur on the island of Streymoy – there was a painting of a ship behind the altar, by Sámal Joensen-Mikines. It was the only time I had ever seen a wholly secular scene displayed behind an altar and the bright blue tones of the painting dazzled the eye among all that white; the sound of the waves outside clearly audible.

As in Iceland, there are no trees on the Faroes. At Norðagøta on the island of Eystroy, we were told that the tiny church there had been constructed from wood salvaged from a shipwreck; jigsawed together to make something new. We all sat down inside it for a while and I tried to imagine these timbers that surrounded us when they were a boat: if some biblical flood had come, we could have tried to change the church back into a ship again and trust that it would bear us safely aloft over the rising waters.

There was a folk museum in the same village, Blasastova; an old farmhouse which had been preserved after the last inhabitants died to show how people had once lived on the Faroes, not very long ago.

It had been a long day, and, one by one, the other journalists in our party thanked the guide and faded out of the museum, to have a little downtime before the next stop. I stayed there, listening. I knew I wouldn't be able to use any of what he said in my article, but he was a compelling storyteller, and I was still slightly entranced by the earlier experience of sitting in the nearby church that had once been a ship.

We had already been told that housing was expensive in the Faroes, and that often households were composed of extended family members.

'There was a local woman who did not have family, and the people in this farmhouse took her in,' the guide said. 'She was a little, how do you say it?' and indicated his head. 'She had only one possession to bring with her. This.'

He pointed to a kind of home-made wooden stool. It was part of a treetrunk that looked as if someone had cut it in a lopsided way. A second piece of wood had been added to make it into a stool; the original piece of wood itself provided support on one side. 'She found the wood washed up on the shore and got it made into a stool. It was the only thing she owned.'

I stared at the crudely made stool. 'One day, the King of Denmark came to visit.' He meant King Frederick IX, who reigned from 1947 until 1972; the Faroes are a self-governing part of the Danish kingdom. 'He called to this house. He offered to buy the stool from her, for 100 gold guineas. She told him she would not sell it even for one guinea.'

I listened, enthralled. I could see the kindness that had been intended by the king; a substantial gift of money to someone who so clearly needed it, in exchange for the only thing she truly prized. But he would not have known that. She did not know the difference between one guinea and one hundred, but she knew the value to her of what she loved: her one possession in life that she would not part with, even to a king.

'How long ago was this?' I said eventually.

'Within living memory.'

'Are there people still in Norðagøta who remember her?'

'Yes.'

And then our guide came to fetch me and I got back on to our bus and we drove away from Norðagøta and the story of the woman who had refused to sell the only thing she owned, although she had been offered a king's ransom in gold for it.

It was too late in the year to see the Northern Lights, but on my third day in Iceland, I went on the Golden Circle bus tour, the most popular day tour out of Reykjavik.

The tundra had the effect of a punch to the eye almost as soon as we left the city. There was so much of it, in all its fierce, savage, wild beauty. I stared out the window, mesmerized by the power of the landscape. The snow still lay on the volcanoes. I was lost in dreaming, suspended over the tundra like a hovering bird, when something the guide said snapped my attention back to the inside of the bus.

'And over there is Thrihnukagigir. It is an extinct volcano.' She pointed out the window, at a location to our right. 'You can go down inside the crater now, in a basket.' You could indeed go there, but it was not part of our tour. How had I missed this in my research? How had I missed the opportunity to descend into a volcano? It was like something out of Jules Verne and his journey to the centre of the earth.

In Guatemala, I had once paid five dollars for a bus ticket to visit Volcán Pacaya which had erupted only six months previously. The bus had picked me and other tourists up from our guesthouses, and brought us some hours' distance to the edge of the lava field. We were told when the bus would be leaving, and were then left to ourselves.

We climbed up towards the crater, huge lines of fire dribbling fiercely down the sides of the volcano. Under our feet, the red-hot lava ran beneath the pumice rock, coming in and out of sight, like some mythical subterranean glowing river. The whole terrain was of fragmented black pumice; old lava.

'This is the best five dollars I have ever spent on anything,' the man I was climbing with said, in what was probably the biggest understatement I have ever heard about anything in my life.

It was crazy, and definitely a bit dangerous, and any official tourist board would have lost their minds about the fact that tourists were being encouraged to climb an active volcano, but it was also utterly thrilling. We had known to wear our hiking boots, but some less-prepared tourists soon had their flip-flops torn to shreds by the sharp black lava. We helped a few of them to go down, and then continued on ourselves. We had to keep moving, because if you stayed still too long, the heat began to penetrate to the soles of your feet: it was literally coming up from the tributaries of lava flowing under the mosaic of pumice.

Every now and then, I received a blast of ferociously hot air to my face, as when you absent-mindedly open a too-hot oven and have your face too close to it. Even though it had been months since the volcano had last erupted, the lava flow was still continuing to dribble down from the crater. As for the stuff that had made it down the slopes and now remained red-hot pooled among the pumice we were walking and running over, it was like the embers of the biggest, hottest fire you could ever imagine in your fireplace: embers that were not contained within a hearth, but were all over the slopes of Volcán Pacaya.

In the end, the two of us turned and ran back down together, holding hands. The heat had got too much for us to remain on the fiery slopes any longer. On the bus back, we all talked a lot, feeling wild and slightly demented. A couple of people were even crying; in shock at the madness of being let loose, unprepared and unguided, to wander on an active lava field. I was utterly exhilarated, half out of my mind with a combination of joy and adrenaline.

If you think that sounds dramatic, you should see some of the videos tourists used to post on YouTube. We saw mere puddles of lava compared to some of the rivers that ran at speed in the distance. You can't climb Volcán Pacaya without a guide any more, and you can't go near the lava itself either. The Guatemalan authorities finally started to regulate the site a couple of years ago. You're unlikely to find the soles of your footwear melting any more as you ascend, and that makes me feel infeasibly sad. I'm just glad that at least once in my life I did something a bit dangerous and a bit crazy.

And now here I was in Iceland, and I was missing the chance to actually go down inside an extinct volcano. Later, I consoled myself with the fact that the tours down the 120 metres into the crater did not run very often. I told myself I could always come back.

'You see those rocks?' our guide asked. She was pointing to large stones near the road we were on. I looked at them. 'Elves live there,' she announced, matter-of-factly. 'They cannot be disturbed. So the road had to be built around them. Such things happen regularly across Iceland. The last time was six weeks ago.'

I turned in my seat to look back at the dwelling place of the elves. I was both intrigued and taken aback by that matter-of-fact tone in her voice. It was as if she really believed elves existed. I come from a country where our most famous souvenir depicts something that definitely doesn't exist: a leprechaun, which most people would think is not far off what an Icelandic elf is. I had been on plenty of Irish tour buses for various stories I was reporting on. There had been many mentions of leprechauns by guides, and all of them delivered in a wholly knowing fashion. My brother, who lives in Kerry, had once told me a story he'd heard from a friend of his who was working in tourism. A tourist bus had stopped in the Iveragh Peninsula between towns and the guide had got out. He had made a kind of pantomime of appearing to talk to something invisible, then leaned down, extended his hand and walked carefully to the other side of the road before standing up straight again, and waving.

'Sir, can I ask what you were doing just now?' one of the American tourists asked when the guide had boarded the bus and it was again in motion.

'Helping a leprechaun to cross the road.'

At our next stop, I went to talk to the guide. Her name was Freyja.

'Can you please tell me what an elf looks like?' I asked. My expression was entirely neutral. I wondered if she would start laughing, or wink at me, or in some way communicate how ridiculous she found my question, because of course elves did not exist.

Freyja did none of those things. She regarded me with unsmiling solemnity. 'They look a lot like us, but more beautiful, and much smaller and they have no [she pointed to her philtrum, the space between the two tiny lines that run between nose and upper lip] whatever that is called in English,' she said earnestly, and without hesitation.

I did not know what to say. She sounded so authentic, so believable, and the detail about the lack of a philtrum was both oddly convincing and somehow unsettling in its random precision. But elves did not exist, any more than leprechauns. Or did they?

Our main stop on the Golden Circle tour was at Gullfoss, which means Golden Falls. We walked across the tundra for some distance, and then climbed some steps. It was cold and clear, and again I marvelled at how my eyesight in Iceland appeared to have dramatically improved since arrival.

I was not prepared for the first sight of Gullfoss. From where we had been walking, nothing was visible, although we could hear huge crashing sounds. Most waterfalls demand to be looked up at. But this one you looked down on; stared down into a huge maw of roaring, churning water so simultaneously violent and stunning that I found I was actually holding my breath.

A series of waterfalls hurl themselves over the volcanic rock, the water coming from the river Hvítá. It takes a while just to figure out their sheer size. The cumulative effect is incredible. I stared and stared. It was so powerful, so beautiful, so intense. There was nothing in the slightest bit pastoral about this waterfall. It was the quintessence of extreme wildness and wilderness.

The land is now in the care of the Icelandic government, but once it formed part of the sheep farm of a man named Tómas Tómasson; an ordinary sheep farm in every sense, except that his land also included this extraordinary waterfall. One of his daughters was Sigríður, born in 1874. Along with her sisters, from time to time as a child, she guided visitors across their sheep farm, along the paths they knew as intimately as lines in the palms of their own hands; visitors from around the world who had heard stories of this astonishing natural phenomenon and wished to see it for themselves. She remained living at the family farmhouse her whole life, until her death in 1957.

Freyja showed us the plaque near the waterfall that had been put there in Sigríður Tómasdóttir's memory. She also told us how Sigríður had, as an adult, campaigned for the land not to be sold to foreign investors who wished to build a hydro-electric plant there. 'She threatened to throw herself into the waterfall if it was to be dammed,' our guide who believed in elves told us. As a result of Sigríður's campaigning, so she said, the Icelandic government eventually bought the land so that Gullfoss could be protected for everyone who wished to see it as the force of nature it is.

The plaque in her memory is asymmetric; seven-sided. It reminded me of one of the jigsaw pieces from the Eastern street scene. Sigríður looks fierce and formidable in it, her jaw set hard in profile, her eye steely, her long plaits like fishing ropes; an environmental heroine.

Later, I researched a bit more into her story. This is what came up when I googled her name. 'Sigríður Tómasdóttir is often credited with having "saved" Gullfoss, an interpretation avidly exploited by the tourist industry,' a stern little entry informed me. 'Although it is widely believed, the very popular story that Sigríður saved the waterfall is untrue . . . But she is still widely regarded as Iceland's first environmentalist.'

She did campaign to save the waterfall, but there were other people ultimately involved. At first, I was keenly disappointed that the story of Sigríður saving Gullfoss for posterity by herself appeared not to be true. But then I decided that that part of her story didn't matter to me. What mattered was the fact that when Sigríður Tómasdóttir was a little girl, she had an actual fairytale landscape to go and look at. It was she and her sisters who took visitors to see their very own waterfall on their own land. She knew the sound of it like the sound of her own voice.

What did that do for your imagination – growing up beside such a fantastical example of how staggeringly spellbinding the natural world could be? Some children grow up with dogs or dolls or particular books or imaginary friends or freedom-giving bicycles as their childhood anchors and landmarks. I had had a beloved imaginary dog and a vast actual library. Sigríður Tómasdóttir had grown up with her own waterfall and it had made her who she became, just as my imagination and my books eventually shaped the person I became.

When I had come back to Ireland after Lewis and I broke off our engagement, I brought the little jigsaw box with me. I kept it safe on a shelf in my living room. I never made the puzzle again, and nor did anyone else. Until now. More than twenty years have passed since Lewis and I made that testing little jigsaw together. This time, I made it on my own. It took an hour and a half, although there are only 119 pieces. It was both as clever and as difficult as I had remembered.

I had never been able to recall what the initials hidden within the jigsaw were. They were larger than I recalled, and located in the sky part of the picture. Whoever the person was who made this beautiful thing back in 1961, their initials were F. S.

When I had finished making the jigsaw by myself, I sat at the table for a while looking at it, remembering our long-ago attic flat in Leeds, and two lives that could have gone in a different direction. I thought of the Snow Queen, and of the Mirror of Understanding and of Kai unsuccessfully trying so hard to complete his ice puzzle; trying so hard to make the word that spelt Eternity.

Bali
2016

VOLITANT

- able to fly

ON NEW YEAR'S DAY, 2016, a minibus from the port of Padang Bai dropped me at the Coco Supermarket at the south end of the gloriously named Monkey Forest Road, in Ubud, Bali. I started walking up Monkey Forest Road, rucksack on my back, sweating profusely. It was late afternoon and the humidity was higher than any I'd ever experienced. I was in search of a guesthouse called Narasoma, at the far end of this road.

The pavements were the usual mosaic of broken tiles, open sewers, and uneven paving stones, some of which had already split neatly in half. That was when I was able to walk on the pavement. Long stretches were occupied by parked motorbikes, or 'motos' as everyone called them.

Their drivers sat alongside, chanting what I soon came to know was the Ubud mantra: 'Taxi? Taxi? You want taxi?' Some drivers who were fed up saying Taxi a thousand times a day simply held up laminated signs instead, which proclaimed in capital letters, 'TAXI'. The noise of the traffic, and the motos and the tourist buses that poured into Ubud every day, was almost physical, it occupied such a large space in the narrow street.

January is usually the start of the wet season in Bali. It was late this year and the humidity and heat were exceptional. My little rucksack was not heavy, at just under 10 kilos, but in that solid heat, it felt like a sack of bricks.

I loved my rucksack almost as much as I loved my passports. It was the same one I'd had for exactly half my life. I had bought it in Covent Garden the summer before I set off on a three-month hitch-hiking journey around the coast of Ireland, in the wet winter of 1990, when I was twenty-five.

My ancient Berghaus had once been a startling shade of violet and jade green. I had never given it a name because I don't like naming inanimate things, but in the days when it was fresh and new and the colours still vivid, I had thought of it as a kind of bird of paradise on my back. Now its feathers were faded and fraying in several places, with a large and permanent brown stain on one side pocket, where the bottle of iodine I'd been carrying to purify water had leaked. One shoulder strap had split at the seams, and I had sewn it together so often with black waxed thread that it looked like a piece of Frankenstein's monster. The hip strap was not padded, as is the norm these days, and sometimes, like now, it dug sharply into my hip bones. The whole thing was as familiar to me as a carapace.

That rucksack owed me nothing, as the phrase went. The truth was, it was completely knackered and really needed to be replaced. I had considered buying a new one for this six-month journey I was now in the middle of, but in the end I just couldn't do it. We went way back, me and that rucksack. We were travel buddies.

Ever since I had bought it in my twenties, and after all those miles I had now travelled, my rucksack had remained a steadfast entity. Amazingly, it had never been stolen along the way or lost in transit. For so long, it had been a reassuring presence emerging on every baggage carousel at all those airports.

It was there every morning in every hostel or tent or cabin or guesthouse or hotel room I had woken up in on my travels.

It had been in Pakistan with me. In Antarctica. In Nepal, and India and Iran. In Mexico and Guatemala. In Hungary, China, Laos and New Zealand and Japan and Bhutan and Cambodia and Vietnam. In Turkey and Ecuador and Colombia and Bolivia and Cuba and Chile, and all the many other places *fernweh* had taken me over all those years. It had become part of my travelling self. I wanted to bring it on one last trip.

I had come that morning from the Gili Islands that lie east of Bali. The boat from Gili Menlo had stopped at Gili Trewanga for an hour, and I had used the time to search for a guesthouse in inland Ubud, where I had never been before. I googled 'Ubud', 'guesthouse' and 'pool'. One of the many places that had come up was a guesthouse called Narasoma. I tried to find an image of its pool, but then realized it was almost time for the ferry to depart.

The entrance to Narasoma was at the far end of Monkey Forest Road, opposite a football field, its surface pitted and rough; this didn't deter the children gleefully playing there. There were signs for it and other guesthouses at the start of Beji Lane; a pedestrian lane it shared with motos, but nothing bigger. I followed it past a second-hand bookshop and traders selling clothes to where a surprisingly large rice field lay opposite the entrance.

It was no more than 25 metres from the frenzied urban chaos of the Ubud traffic on Monkey Forest Road to Narasoma's pastoral, bucolic entrance; a fact that never failed to astonish me in the weeks to come as they represented totally different worlds and habitats.

I stepped into the little open-air reception area, with its beautiful carved wooden arches.

'You have a reservation?' Desak, the woman behind the desk, asked me.

'No.'

She consulted a ledger. 'We have a room,' she declared. 'I will show it to you. How long will you stay?'

'Three days?' I offered. I never stay anywhere long. What I love is feeling the miles endlessly unscrolling beneath my feet: packing up my rucksack every few days and moving on to the next place, the next guesthouse, the next new experience.

She took a key and indicated that I was to follow.

'Excuse me,' I said. 'Could I see the pool first?'

We walked through a large jungly courtyard and along a twisting path that ran between two high walls. Suddenly, the space opened out. I was looking down into a vast hollow, an immense green space, where coconut trees rose high into the sky like the masts of verdant ships. There was a bridge, and a river running through the space. There were banana trees, frangipani trees with lemon-coloured blossoms, and a tree I later discovered was a very old durian.

In the middle of all this impossibly tumbling lush greenness was an empty infinity pool, fringed with pink hibiscus at one end. From above, I could see the steps that led into that blue water. It was the kind of pool you usually only see in a five-star hotel, but this was not even a hotel, it was a guesthouse where my room cost the equivalent of €25 a night. It was a perfect pool in a perfect environment; a pool that I had been longing to swim in all my life. I stared down at it, and my heart lurched with joy.

In the beginning, when I had gone travelling for several months at a time, it was because I was in between jobs, or worked freelance. When I got a proper job, I managed to periodically take advantage of the unpaid leave that was available to staff. There was never any reason, other than the perpetual pull of fernweh.

This time was different. The previous year, a decade-long attempt to become a parent via adoption had come to an end. I had aged out while waiting, as the blunt expression went. Parenthood was not going to happen for me in any form. It was then that I went to seek time off. I felt an overwhelming visceral need to put time and space and distance between what I had hoped for so long that my life would be, and what I knew it now was going to be: one without parenthood. I knew the only place I could make that essential transition in my head was elsewhere.

I didn't have to explain to the then editor why I wanted time off. He had read the in-depth story I'd written about how, due to confusing changes to Irish state legislation in 2010, inter-country adoption in Ireland had collapsed for many potential adoptive parents; a cohort that included me. I had put myself into the story to maximize its impact. I rarely shared personal information about my own life with readers, but after much thought, I had decided there was no shame in publicly stating how much I hoped and wanted to be a parent.

When the story came out, it did focus national attention on something very few people knew about, and it did act as a piece of public service journalism. But it made no difference to my own situation. Nothing can change the fact that you're getting older every day. After almost ten years of endless paperwork, of scores of hours of assessments by social workers, and home visits, of having my medical details and financial details and (lack of) criminal record examined every year, and my guardians and referees being re-interviewed every time the paperwork expired, I had finally withdrawn my application.

I knew I needed to get away from Dublin then; far away from my life in Ireland, so I could mend and recover in the place I loved best: elsewhere. But it was taking much longer than I had anticipated to get my request for unpaid leave signed off. Reasons filtered down to me. I was needed. Our resources in the features department – that meant people – were limited. Apparently, the paper was in a period of transition, so now wasn't a good time, although if there is one thing I definitely know from working on a daily national paper for more than two decades, it is that we are perpetually in a period of transition.

One day, distraught at the prospect that this leave might not be granted, I stood in the editor's office and spoke with uncharacteristic bluntness. I pointed out that if my adoption had come about, not only would I not be in the office for several months, but I would be on paid leave and, furthermore, I would then have used the additional unpaid leave period available to parents under European law, and these things would have happened no matter how stretched our resources were, or how much transition we were undergoing. That I was never going to be a parent now, and I needed time to adjust and mourn this fact.

It was an unconventional approach, and I don't know which of us found that conversation more excruciating, but my unpaid leave eventually came about; a fact for which I was profoundly grateful to the paper, and still am. And now it was New Year's Day; the first day of a new year, and a new beginning in a new elsewhere.

I did not document my travels via any social media when on the road, but every now and then I wrote a long group email to family and friends. The one I sent some time after arriving in Ubud was headed, 'My Bali Coma in Narasoma, aka Paradise'. It was only half a joke. After my three days were up, I had gone back to Desak at reception, booked in for a further six weeks, and set about extending my Indonesian visa. For once, I didn't want to go anywhere else. The road was not calling me ever onwards. I had found what for me felt like a perfect place.

So many people had told me Bali had long since been ruined, and that Ubud was a rubbish-strewn noisy traffic hellhole that had once been lovely, but was now also ruined. It was true that if you came only for a day trip, as many tourists did, your impression would be almost wholly of the traffic nightmare of Monkey Forest Road, and over-eager hawkers in the markets, but Ubud was different when you were staying there.

I loved its temples, and markets and galleries, and cafés and water palace and textile shops: but what I loved most of all about it was my base at Narasoma. It was an improbable rural idyll right in the middle of an urban centre: like finding a guesthouse surrounded by fields and wildlife less than twenty steps from Grafton Street. Literally one minute I was in the thick of sirens and weaving motos and noise and broken pavements, and inside that same minute I was staring at the rice field opposite Narasoma's entrance which had been a mere inch or two high when I arrived and was now growing by the green minute.

There were twenty-two rooms scattered around the compound, some of them in various traditional wooden buildings, three of which had been imported from Java. My room, Marigold, was in the main building. The rooms there were all named after the flowers that grew so abundantly everywhere: marigold, frangipani, gardenia, lotus, rose, lily, champaca. Each one had a large Balinese painting of the flower the room was named after: my marigold painting shone like a domesticated sun in one corner.

My room had dual-aspect balconies, a marble floor, a rattan ceiling, a family of geckos, a large bed with a mosquito net, a beautifully carved teak wardrobe, and a desk and stool. There was an adjoining modest bathroom, partly open to the elements. I loved this room; the sound of the gamelan that I could hear in the courtyard below during the day, and in the evening the cheesy songs that carried in from Alit's warung beside us in the laneway: 'Summertime', 'The Girl from Ipanema', 'Que Sera Sera'. In the evenings too, the frog chorus started. The frogs lived in the rice fields, and on my way back to Narasoma in the evenings, I always stopped to listen to their unseen orchestra.

In the mornings, I had fresh pineapple juice, Balinese coffee and nasi goreng, in an open-sided bale overlooking the pool. My mornings started long before breakfast – usually at dawn, about 6.30, when I woke and went straight down to the pool. At that time of day, I almost always had it to myself.

I swam up and down in a blissful daze, as the coconut trees occasionally dropped their lethal cargo with a distant crash, and the bright birds swooped down to the water, and the lizards came out to bask in the early sun, and the fat little tropical squirrels with their flat, beaver-like tails scampered up and down the trees. It was sixteen strokes from end to end. I swam for at least an hour in the morning, an hour later in the day, and often for another hour before dusk fell at about 6 p.m. In the evenings, flocks of white egrets flew overhead, their wings folding and unfolding like silken parasols.

It became my ritual to swim there, necessary in a way I couldn't explain even to myself. It wasn't just the heat that drew me; it was simple pure joy. I began to crave the pool, even when I was out in Ubud, having lunch or dinner or drinks with the friends I had made since arriving. At the Three Monkeys or the Thai warung on the street I nicknamed Restaurant Alley, or at Toro Sushi, or Ibu Oka, or at Cinema Paradiso, or at Sari out in the rice fields, or wherever we were that day, I held the image of the blue surface of the Narasoma pool in my head like a promise.

It was Charlotte who told me that much of the Narasoma land had been bought from the Ubud Palace at the top of Monkey Forest Road, where dancers performed each evening. Charlotte was the co-owner of Narasoma, with her Balinese husband, Nyoman: they had met in Australia years before. There was an actual monkey forest at the other end of Monkey Forest Road, where bored monkeys stole tourists' sunglasses and whatever food they were foolish enough to have on them.

Rice fields were stitched into the most unlikely places in Ubud: at the side of restaurants, opposite Narasoma, behind warungs and at the end of lanes. There had been far more of these in the past, but the rice fields in the centre of Ubud that gave it so much of its charm were slowly being sold off so that more guesthouses and restaurants could be built on them. The unspoilt jungle that made Narasoma so special was the last remaining part of the original monkey forest that had once stretched from Ubud Palace to where the monkey forest had now shrunk to. I had never once seen a monkey in the Narasoma compound, and said so to Charlotte.

'When we bought the land, I took some offerings down there,' she said. She meant the beautiful handmade little baskets woven from grasses and filled with flowers and rice that the Balinese place at thresholds twice a day, and then wave incense over them. 'The monkeys came to see who had bought the land.'

'What do you mean?'

'The day we bought the land, two clans of monkeys arrived to see who had bought their old land,' she said. 'There were about twenty in each, with little ones too.'

The monkeys, having inspected the new owners and approved, then departed and never returned.

Ubud was an unashamedly hedonistic place. I swam, ate, read, swam, and hung out with the friends I had made: Australians Susanna and her son Maxim; Diana, Naomi; Pierre Louis, a Parisian; Ali from Wales and on the road five full years; Susan from Boston; Matt and Alison, originally from England and almost two decades working in China. I had never done so little when out on the road. In a jewellery shop crammed with silver and moonstones and amethysts, I bought a ring with a blue topaz stone from Borneo the exact colour of the Narasoma swimming pool, and did not take it off.

In the house I grew up in, my father had a study filled with books. It was a room that received sun, and I spent many afternoons of my childhood in there before he came home from work, lying on the pale green carpet in the sunlight like a dozy cat, reading my own books. His books – history, policy, biographies – were far too complicated and opaque for me to be interested in.

What I did constantly refer to were the bright stacks of holiday brochures piled up on a lower shelf behind the door. They changed as the seasons came and went, but there was always a satisfyingly substantial pile of them, the pages glossy and gaudy with colour.

The brochures were for package holidays in Europe. My father travelled a lot for work and made his arrangements with a local travel agent, who must have given these to him. I spent hours and hours looking through these brochures. I could not get enough of them. Most of the photographs in the brochures were of hotels. There were the occasional pictures of beaches with parasols and palm trees, but the majority of the content was of hotels. I looked at endless pictures of lobbies and reception desks, empty hotel bedrooms with doors open to balconies, restaurants with long buffet tables covered in white tablecloths, ballrooms and corridors and foyers full of armchairs where nobody sat. These hotels perpetually awaited their guests, and I liked to imagine that one day, those guests might include our family.

But much as I loved to study the photographs of the dining rooms and carpeted lobbies and bedrooms, with their exotic balconies to the open air, the true joy for me were the swimming pools. Every hotel showed pictures of its swimming pool. There were turquoise blue lozenges under an equally blue sky, there were oval pools, there were round pools, there were the occasional asymmetrical pools. Sometimes there were two pools looking like a figure of eight, with a pedestrian bridge arching over them, or pools with little islands in the middle, waterfalls tumbling over piled rocks. What they all had in common was that clarity of blue and lightness, the surfaces shimmering with tantalizing promise.

These swimming pools fascinated me through the afternoons of my childhood. I recall all these pools being empty, although many had chairs and sunbeds and umbrellas nearby, as if the people who had been occupying them had just gone inside. The surfaces of the pools were calm and unbroken, like solid, perfect pieces of ice.

The outdoor swimming pools looked cerulean under the kind of vast blue skies I rarely saw in the west of Ireland, where the sky I knew was mercurial and frequently grey. It was not the unbroken blue canopy of the brochures. Sometimes, along with the parasols, there were trees with frothy clouds of pink and white flowers in the background; flowers as exotic and unlikely to me as parrots.

I studied the steps down into the brochure pools, always wondering how deep they were, and how many strokes it would take to get across those perfect blue rectangles; fantasizing about what it would feel like to have the hot sun over my body and the cool water around and underneath me.

I could not swim. We went each summer until I was eleven on holiday to Co. Kerry, where there was a beautiful sandy beach at Derrynane, and a stony one at Bealtra. My father could not swim either. I never saw him in swimming trunks. I recall my mother paddling in the sea just once, in an electric-blue costume trimmed with orange flowers that I didn't see again. She could not swim either.

On those Kerry beaches, I paddled cautiously in the shallows, longing to go further out. It seemed to me that people could either swim by some instinct or they couldn't, and I couldn't. My school did not have swimming lessons, and it never occurred to me to ask for my own lessons. I had never been in a swimming pool, or even seen one in real life.

Sometimes in the ocean in Kerry, I would take my feet off the bottom and flail about, hoping this time I would suddenly, miraculously stay afloat, but every time, my body began to pull me steadily downwards. Every time, I felt a sharp pang of renewed deep disappointment; an unshakeable feeling that no matter how many times I tried, my body would never be the buoyant entity I longed for, but would betray me with this inexorable downward tug.

Over time, I had finally figured out how to respond when people asked me if I had children.

'No. But not for lack of trying,' I would reply calmly, right back at them, my expression neutral. That was just enough information for the questions to cease. In the beginning, I had merely said, 'No,' and hoped the grilling would end there. Sometimes it didn't. Once, at a party, a woman I had never met before collared me and asked the children question. I replied in the negative. Then she said, 'Oh well, you must have pets, then. A dog?'

The party was in a basement bar in Dublin, and the room was dim, a fact I was grateful for, because I knew my expression was one of contempt.

'I don't have a dog,' I said. I wanted to smack her.

'You must have a cat, then. Surely you have a cat?'

My contempt was turning to unexpected distress. Were women like me who didn't have children automatically assumed to be crazy cat ladies, whatever that pejorative term meant? Did this person making outrageous assumptions about my childless status think of course I must have a dog or a cat or who knows what kind of creature as some sort of substitute for a human child? In my distress, I thought: is this what my life has come to? Being second-guessed and judged in this humiliating way?

'I don't have a fucking cat,' I hissed, and then walked away, leaving the woman with her mouth agape.

In truth, this kind of thing never stops for women. The assumptions people sometimes make about your visible childlessness often catch you off guard. Years ago, a close friend of mine in Dublin was having a lunch for her women friends the week before she got married. I was there. After the lunch itself, people lingered on as arranged, having cocktails and chatting. I was the first to leave. I excused myself, saying I had to go on somewhere. As I got up, one of the other women, whom I barely knew, joked that I was so lucky to be having two social outings in one afternoon; whereas she was on the clock with her husband to get home to their small baby.

The friend whose lunch it was arrowed a glance at me. I had told her in advance why I would have to leave early: I had to attend the annual general meeting of the International Adoption Association of Ireland, an organization of which I was a member. All members knew it would be a wholly depressing gathering, because the inter-country adoption system in Ireland had been in legislative paralysis for some years. I said my goodbyes lightly enough, but on the bus journey out of town to the venue, in some awful soulless airport hotel by a roundabout, I put my hands up to my face and cried.

If you remember nothing else about this book, please remember this: don't ask people you don't know if they have children. This question, I have observed over many years, is usually asked only by those who already have children. Of course there are also people who are happily childless by choice, but again in my experience, this cohort are quite proactive in volunteering that information themselves. Individuals like me who don't have children never ask that particular question of others: we know there are frequently painful reasons for childlessness.

There is no polite way to put this, but truthfully, it really is none of your business asking such a deeply personal question of people you don't know.

Our family never did go on a holiday together out of Ireland to one of those hotels and swimming pools I spent so much time examining in my father's brochures, but by the time I was nineteen, I had started travelling myself. As I'd got older, I had become too embarrassed to admit I could not swim. I still loved being by the water, and I would splash around in the shallows, or lie down on the beach and let the water wash over me, but by the time I arrived in Australia aged twenty-two, I remained unable to swim.

I lived in Sydney for the first five months of that Australian year. One of my Australian housemates in the shared house in Enmore was a girl called Cath. It was Cath and her sister Jack who took me under their Australian wings and invited me out with them and their many friends on the weekend expeditions they were always going on.

We went bushwalking; we brought rugs and picnics and sat outdoors in Sydney parks listening to open-air opera, at one of which Joan Sutherland sang; we went to the barbecues that were constantly happening at people's houses; we went to parties and shopped at markets that sold exotic things like Balinese sarongs and vintage clothes, and we were always, always, always, going to the beach.

I managed to hide the fact that I could not swim. I arrived during winter, which felt hotter to me than summers in Ireland. To me, the water of the Pacific Ocean was astonishingly warm, although my new Australian friends deemed it cold. I stayed in the ocean at Coogee and Maroubra beaches longer than they did, horsing around in the shallows, the sky so bright my eyes hurt.

One weekend, Cath loaded up her Ute and a group of us went to picnic and swim at a lake somewhere north of Sydney. When we got there, we discovered that there was a tyre tied to a tree that overhung the lake. Our party took turns swinging on it, letting go, and jumping down into the water. I looked on from a distance, and managed to evade my turn without anyone noticing.

At some point that afternoon, a decision was made to swim across the lake and picnic there instead. As I watched in silent horror, the picnic was divided up among several plastic bags and boxes, and people started to swim across, balancing their cargo easily on their heads, swapping arms from time to time. I remained on the shoreline. The first people across were already starting to set up. They called over to us to hurry up, and their words ricocheted and echoed across the lake.

'Are you ready?' Cath enquired, waving across at others in the party. Cath, of course, could swim as easily as she could walk or run.

'I can't swim,' I confessed flatly. In this situation, there was no concealing the fact any more.

'Of course you can,' Cath said in amazement. 'Everyone can swim.'

'No, I really can't,' I insisted, panicked now at the thought of being forced into deep water just so I could prove my inability to stay afloat.

'I'll teach you,' Cath announced. 'Get in the water.'

'Get in the water?' I repeated blankly. 'Why?'

'Because I'm going to teach you to swim.'

I stared at her. 'Now?'

'Now,' Cath said briskly. 'I've done a life-saving course, so you are not going to drown.'

But I can't swim, I thought. I entered the water with dread, and slowly waded out after Cath.

'Keep going,' Cath said. 'Stop.' The water was at my armpits. 'First, you learn how to tread water, so you can have a rest when you start swimming across the lake.' And then she began to instruct me.

I am not sure what happened that day. Did I trust Cath because she had done a life-saving course? Because I didn't want to lose any more face than I already had? Or because the water was warm, and easy to remain in for a long time?

However it came about, an ordinary and extraordinary miracle happened: I was finally afloat. I could tread water. I could do breaststroke. Cath beside me, I swam across that lake and back, feeling as if I was doing something as improbable as flying. I was a wholly inelegant swimmer, but all that mattered to me was that I was no longer sinking when I went out of my depth, and I was actually going somewhere at last. It was a glorious and unforgettable sensation of suddenly being something like invincible.

By the time I got to Bali, it was several years since Elizabeth Gilbert's famous book, which is partly set there, had been published. *Eat, Pray, Love: One Woman's Search for Everything across Italy, India and Indonesia*, was referred to colloquially in Ubud as 'the book'. 'Eat, Pray, Leave' read the slogans on T-shirts. 'Feed, Spay, Love' was the sign over a veterinary clinic. 'Eat, Pray, Stay' read a sign over more than one guesthouse.

I had never read the book, or seen the movie, but when browsing one day in Igna, the tatty bookshop at the top of Beji

Lane, I found a second-hand copy. I read it in a day. I could see why so many people had loved it: the escapism, the narrative, and the fact that Gilbert was a damn good writer. The section I liked most was in Italy; she wrote beautifully and compellingly about food. As it happened, since arriving, a few people – all men – had asked me if it was *Eat, Pray, Love* that had brought me to Ubud: apparently single Western women came all the time, looking to emulate something of what Gilbert had found there.

What she found in Ubud in the third and final part of her year travelling after a horrible divorce was, of course, love with another expat. It was undoubtedly the traditional feel-good ending to the book that helped make it irresistible to so many: who among us is not secretly a sucker for happy endings, no matter how societally conservative those are?

I brought *Eat, Pray, Love* back to Igna and part-traded it for another book, as I did with all the books I bought there, but it stayed in my head. Why was it that happy endings for women in books, even those based on a true story, such as Gilbert's, inevitably seemed to involve either romantic love or children, or preferably both? When in reality, many women's lives did not work out that societally prescribed way, for some reason or another?

A couple of months earlier on this trip, I had gone to visit friends in Yangon, Myanmar. Joe and Sarah, old friends from Ireland, were working and living there with their little daughter, Eliza.

On my last night, I suggested that before dinner we all go to visit one of the astrologists who were honeycombed into rooms at the back of Sule Pagoda, a temple that stands islanded among the traffic of downtown Yangon, an absurdly beautiful golden urban obelisk. In the West, we mostly think of astrologists and fortune tellers as barely credible; a clichéd lot who all spout the same things to women about tall dark strangers. In many parts of Asia, fortune tellers are part of everyday life, mainly due to the fact that people go to them for very pragmatic reasons: to learn the state of their future literal economic status.

It was dark by then, and going on for 7 p.m., but the resident astrologists and palmists were still in their little rooms, side by side at the curved back of the pagoda. There were about seven of them, mostly men. Their doors stood open to the evening mosquitoes and the air that was thick with the metallic smells of exhaust and of incense sticks from the pagoda, which drifted over the connecting walls like scented ghosts. They didn't look like the tellers of fates of any kind. They looked, in fact, entirely bureaucratic in their little identical offices, with piles and piles of papers on their desks, and manual typewriters and old filing cabinets in the corners.

'I'm not sure if I'm in the right state of mind for this tonight,' Sarah said, when we had traversed the row of offices, peering through the open doors into each.

'I'm on,' Joe said.

'Me too,' I declared firmly. 'It's my last night.'

We arranged that we would meet Sarah for drinks in a nearby hotel after our readings, and she headed off.

There was only one woman among the line of astrologists, and Joe and I both decided we would choose her. He went in first. I walked up and down the circular pathway outside, wondering why it was I wanted to go and see a fortune teller, when for years the only thing I had really wanted to know about the future was if I would be a parent one day.

But I knew the answer to that now. Suddenly I felt panicky, and sad, and scared. I kept pacing, and my slow funk began to increase. I didn't want to feel like this on my last night with friends I saw so rarely, and liked so much; didn't want to leave them the next day with a stain of sadness having leached into our precious time together. I started to regret my suggestion that we visit an astrologist. I continued to pace up and down, breathing in the exhaust fumes and the incense, waiting for Joe, thinking that when he emerged I would just say that I wasn't, after all, going to do it.

Joe came out beaming; elated and buzzed, waving the piece of paper the astrologist had given him like a sailor bearing a navigation chart. 'That was amazing!' he proclaimed happily. 'So interesting!' He'd ushered me inside before I had time to protest, saying he and Sarah would wait for me in the hotel bar.

The woman in the little office told me to sit down. I sat at the other side of her large desk, my back to the street and the open door. She stared at me, halfway between frowning and smiling. I was her last appointment of the day. I could sense her tiredness. She wanted to go home. Everything in the office was covered in layers of dust, which was routine in Asia. She had a laptop the size of a now obsolete telephone directory. It was hotter inside the office than it had been outside, and the fan churning its blades on the grey filing cabinet made no impact on the heavy air.

She asked me my birthday, and the time of my birth. What was my country? She busied herself at the ancient laptop, doing calculations, which she wrote on a piece of paper. Then she reached across the desk and took both my palms in hers, staring intently at them. Cockroaches started to march across the desk; she ignored them, but I could not. My eyes kept twitching sideways. Mosquitoes and other tiny biting, buzzing insects flew at my face. My hands were being held firmly and I could not brush away the insistent biting insects. I shook my head vigorously, but the buzzing continued.

'Children are too late for you,' she announced. Even though I knew this was true, I thought I might disgrace myself and start crying in public. Start howling. I feared that I'd cast myself down on the dusty floor caked with dead bugs and put my hands over my eyes and sob for hours, as I had done so often in the past.

'You have travelled many times for a long time. How many times you have had long travels?' I told her. 'You will have three' – she corrected herself in mid-flow, as if unsure – 'no, four more long trips and many little trips. Then you must stop.' I'm never stopping, I thought. My rucksack will finally fall apart and be left behind, but I never will. I'll always travel.

'You are patient and kind.' Really? Sometimes. I think I am sometimes patient and kind. Well, maybe not that patient. No, I am. I am patient and kind. Yes, I thought, I'll take that one.

There was more; things about career and money and invest-ments: the fortune bit of fortune telling. Then she stopped. It was over. Relieved, I started to take the 6,000 kyat reading fee out of my purse.

'You want to ask me anything else?'

I hesitated. There was something I wanted to ask, but I also did not want to ask it. Oh, what the hell.

'Yes,' I said. 'Will I fall in love again?' And then, 'Will I get married?' My face burned scarlet. I could not believe what I had just said. This was ridiculous and stupid and juvenile.

'Yes,' she answered without pausing. 'Yes, there is love again for you. But he is not from your country, not from Ireland.' Neither were the other three men I had loved, and who had loved me, I thought philosophically. That was part of the reason why none of those relationships had endured. 'And if you want to marry, that will be OK,' she went on to say. 'But you will also be OK if you don't get married. Do you understand? You will be OK even if you don't get married.' She closed the laptop with a thud, and started gathering her things.

I looked at her in dismay. This was not what I wanted to hear at all. I had wanted a big fat giant unequivocal yes; that I was definitely getting married. I did not want to hear I would be OK unmarried. It was the last thing I wanted to hear. I had never thought of myself as a person who would not get married, but then again, I had never thought of myself as a person who would not have children, and look how that had turned out.

In Ubud, after I had brought *Eat, Pray, Love* back to Igna, and was writing my diary at my desk in Marigold, I thought back to that evening in Yangon a couple of months previously. I realized I too had been unconsciously hoping for someone to tell me there would be an amorphous happy ending for me.

I thought then about shame. There is something that hovers over women like me who don't have children, and who are not married or in a partnership, when they reach a certain stage in life. There must be something essentially wrong with us, is the message that is out there in the ether. The shame message. I have not always lived alone, and I hope some day in the future to again share my life with someone, but right now, I live alone and am not in a partnership. And that carries its own silent stigma and judgement in our society: the almost imperceptible shame that you are both expected and made to feel as a woman in all sorts of subtle ways when you are single, but most particularly when you don't have children.

This almost intangible, insubstantial shame doesn't, in my experience, extend to men who don't have children or a long-term partner. It's specifically women who are judged and found lacking in some way; for having failed some test that I for one never knew we had to take. I'm not sure exactly when or where it began, except it was long ago, and is now so ingrained in all sorts of cultural and societal ways, it's impossible to identify any one origin.

I sat in Marigold at my desk that evening bullishly writing these things in my diary: things I usually never want to think about, because they inevitably brought a sensation of the taint of shame with them, no matter how much I told myself I didn't care how society viewed me.

There had been two miscarriages in the past. Both had happened with a former partner, a Canadian man I had first met when travelling in Central America. Dex and I had met by chance in Mexico. We were having lunch by ourselves at nearby tables in an open-air restaurant, El Panchan, in Palenque, near the Mayan ruins. We had a short, inconsequential conversation about the merits of our guidebooks (his Lonely Planet, mine Footprint), and said goodbye.

At dawn the following morning, Dex turned up as a passenger on my minibus, heading for what turned out to be the next destination for both of us. He took a seat beside me. By the time we got off the minibus for good, we had talked for twelve hours straight. We shouldered our rucksacks, took each other's hand, and walked away as a couple, without ever having to discuss what we would do next. We checked into the first hotel that looked any way reasonable, and went straight to bed.

We were together after that for an extended period, inasmuch as the distance between two continents allowed. Dex had travelled extensively too. We discovered we had some collective memories of being in the same countries, at different times, and we delighted in this shared retrospective experience of our separate elsewheres.

A year or so after our first meeting, we arranged to meet again in Central America, and spent several weeks travelling there. In a town in Guatemala where there were no such things as pregnancy tests for sale, Dex had been the one to go and fetch the results of a blood test after I had seen a doctor in Antigua.

I waited in our room at the guesthouse. The room had insistent cracks down its white-painted walls from former earthquakes. Our window framed a volcano, Volcán de Agua, and as I sat in the wide window seat there, waiting for Dex to come back, I felt as if I was balancing uncertainly on a tightrope. I was between one future and another. I stared and stared at the volcano, and thought: I will never forget these minutes, this waiting, this view.

The door opened. Dex came in, as playful and cheery and utterly reassuring as he always was. He handed the letter to me, and stood close by, watching as I took the piece of paper out of the envelope.

Positive.

We held each other tightly.

Some time later, when we were in San Pedro La Laguna, I went to pee in the bathroom. There was blood when I wiped. I stared down at the piece of white toilet paper, now streaked with scarlet.

There was suddenly an animal noise coming from nearby, a sound I didn't recognize; that I had never heard before. It was me, I slowly registered with the tiny remaining part of my consciousness that wasn't in shock: it was me who was making that ferocious, unstoppable, primal howling sound without even knowing I was creating it. I was crouched down on the ground against the wall by then, my arms folded around my upper body and head.

The lava of grief swiftly poured under the door and spread into the bedroom, where I had left Dex reading on our bed, waiting for me to get ready to go out for dinner.

Two days later, at the tiny makeshift mission hospital in San Pedro, I put on an oversized second-hand T-shirt with a Dunkin' Donuts logo. It had been offered to me in place of the hospital gown their resources did not run to. Dex waited as I went into surgery for dilation and curettage. When I came out later, and we went back into the world of signs for Spanish classes, and two-for-one margaritas, and bootleg film nights; mixing with all the other uncaring, lively, happy tourists who were unknowing of our lost future, I realized I had never fully understood what grief was before.

The second time was when we were living together in Cambridge, Massachusetts. I had been awarded a year-long Nieman Fellowship at the Nieman Foundation for Journalism at Harvard, and as partners could also come for the duration, Dex was there too. I had just reached the twelve-week milestone. I had been given a due date. I had prints of scans, with the name 'Baby Boland' on them. The sonographer had asked me what surname to put on them. I couldn't tell her. Dex and I had been gingerly talking about where we might live in the future; about how we would manage as parents living in two different continents. I couldn't make up my mind about the surname. In the absence of a decision, the sonographer gently suggested that as I was the one under hospital care, she would use mine for those images of our baby.

Dex had fretted when I had shown him the scan pictures. He was afraid for me, and for himself too. He thought it was too early to be joyous, but at twelve weeks, I thought everything was safe: our child, our relationship, our future as a little family.

With the second miscarriage, we went through the same process as the first time, except this time, there were proper gowns at Boston's Brigham and Women's Hospital. The grief, however, was not the same this time: it was worse. I had never known how it could possess every atom of your waking moments, and often find you in the sleeping ones too. I also truly understood for the first time what inconsolable meant.

Dex tried so hard to console me. My sister, at the end of a phone line from Ireland, tried. My very closest friends on the fellowship, in whom I had just recently confided I was pregnant, tried. I had literally nothing to say to any of them; I was silent.

In my state of mind at that time, I felt it was futile talking to anyone, even Dex, who was suffering so much himself, because there was not one thing anyone could say that would make me, or him, feel even the tiniest bit better, because the fact was irrefutable: our baby was dead. At one point in the worst of the immediate aftermath, I found myself actually seriously wondering if I would ever be able to have a normal conversation with anyone ever again.

My consultant called us back in some time later to reassess our chances, and to discuss the results of tests that had been carried out on the tissue. I sat there in a daze and let it all go over my head. I was simply incapable of concentration. I was relying on Dex to remember everything.

'Would you like to know what the gender was?' the consultant asked, out of nowhere.

That penetrated the fog I was in. I stared at her, mute with horror. I had had names in my head for our son or daughter; names I had discussed with Dex. Dante or Kit for a boy, and Lyra or Piper for a girl. They were unusual names, outlandish even, but names I had long loved. People would definitely remember our child's name. But our baby was dead now. And this woman was on the brink of haunting my dreams for the rest of my life with her unwanted information as to whether it was a son or a daughter that we had lost. I knew I would not be able to cope with that information. But no words were coming out of my mouth, and I was terrified of whatever word might come out of hers next. I clutched Dex's hand and started sobbing loudly. The meeting ended shortly after.

When Dex and I left the Brigham on that snowy February afternoon, I did not know it at the time, but that second miscarriage was to be the absolute end of my hope that I would ever have a child. I did not become pregnant again. And when I returned to Ireland and recommenced the adoption process I had put on hold while out of the country, that did not happen either.

Parenthood would never happen for me now. There would be no bedtime stories to read, no birthday cakes I would try my best to bake, no rising marks of height recorded at the same place on the kitchen wall, no small hand in mine, no first day at school, no first everything else forever after, no knowledge of that fierce, overwhelming parental love; no child.

*

Narasoma, in common with many other guesthouses and hotels in Bali, was also a spa. It had a separate building that was a yoga retreat centre. Under the pool, and overlooking the river were a series of tranquil rooms that offered spa treatments. On my desk in Marigold was a leaflet detailing what was on offer at the spa, including six kinds of body scrub.

I could not walk down Monkey Forest Road at any time of day more than a couple of metres before encountering a smiling young woman incanting, 'Massage?' and offering a leaflet. There were literally scores of spas, wellness centres and yoga studios all along Monkey Forest Road, and the other Ubud streets I walked daily. There were a baffling variety of spas, the meaning of whose names were mysteries to me: Shriman Yoga and Vedic Astrology; Intuitive Flow Yoga Studio; Bodyworks Healing Centre; Amrtasiddhi Ayurvedic Health Centre; Conscious Healing Radiantly Alive Yoga Centre; Asian Prophecy Spa. I didn't avail of any of them. I wasn't interested. All I really cared about was the pool.

But even I eventually awoke from my Narasoma Coma and realized that Bali is internationally famous for its spas for a reason. People come from all over the world to learn new massage techniques, or to experience the extraordinary range and variety of treatments there: I had met several of them in the weeks I had spent in Ubud. There were more than 170 spas in and around Ubud alone. I knew it would be a shame to have spent so long there without experiencing anything that was at the core of what many other people came there for. More than that, massage is a deeply important and fundamental part of the Balinese culture, as innately Balinese as the ritual daily offerings or the temples or the wood carvings, all of which I loved.

With only a few days left before my visa extension ran out, I finally sat at my desk in Marigold and applied myself to the internet to do some forensic research. I went at it with the focus I had when on deadline for an assignment. My strategy was simple. I was planning to do a full day of signature treatments at whichever spa the crowd considered to be the best.

A couple of hours later I realized that I had been laughably naïve in thinking I could get anywhere near spending a day in Ubud's best-known spas unless I'd made a booking long, long in advance. I had, however, made some progress in deciding where to go.

The spa that the internet was going wild for was a place called Karsa, a couple of miles out of town, beyond the Campuhan Ridge, and among the rice fields. 'Ubud has hundreds of spas. Why choose us?' its website proclaimed. Why, indeed? Popularity was clearly one reason, because it was nearly impossible to get a booking there. I was going to trust the crowd and let it guide me on a subject I knew nothing of: I decided I wanted to go to Karsa, and have a massage there.

Their website had a long list of treatments, and I had almost no idea what any of them were. What for instance, I wondered, was a 'Singing Bowl Healing Vibration'? The description said that the bowl had been 'forged under a full moon in Nepal'. (*Yeah, right,* I found myself automatically thinking, before scolding myself for being so literal.) 'Our male therapists have learned to work with the "vibratory energies" of the bowl.' During treatment, the bowl 'is placed over energy centres and acupressure points on your back, shoulders, legs and feet then struck as well as rubbed, to produce two different types of vibration and sound.'

This is the kind of thing that makes me feel queasy to read. I don't believe that healing vibration – whatever that is – comes from a singing bowl, no matter where it was forged, or what kind of light it was made in. It's like being asked to believe in God, and I don't. But here I was, in Ubud, and I was damn well going to make sure I did not miss out on the experience of having a massage here.

I read on. I decided I would remain under the guidance of the crowd when choosing my treatment. According to Karsa, their most popular massage was one called an 'Intuitive Heart Massage'; a 90-minute treatment for 270,000 Indonesian rupiah, the equivalent of €18.

The thing was, according to their website, there was not a single session open for the few days remaining of my time in Ubud. I was not giving up. I called them.

I named the day when I would be leaving the country, three days hence. 'I was wondering if you might have any openings between now and then?' I asked.

'You have no booking?'

'I have no booking.'

There was a long pause. I held the phone and stared out at one of the temples, against which strings of marigolds punched out their startling colour. It was the first time I had admitted to myself I was actually leaving. By now, the rice in the fields opposite Narasoma, a mere inch when I had arrived, was knee high. I was going on to see half a dozen close friends in the US for the last leg of this journey; friends from Harvard whom we collectively jokingly referred to as 'sisters and brothers by other mothers and fathers', because we had spent so much time together in our fellowship year. Although I was hugely looking forward to seeing them, almost all of me did not want to leave Marigold, or Nara-soma, or Ubud, or Bali.

'Madame?'

'Yes?'

'You are lucky. We have had a cancellation this morning.'

There was one free slot in the coming days. It was for ninety minutes on the day before I was due to depart. I booked the choice of the crowd: the intuitive heart massage.

A few days later, I set off to walk the hour or so it was going to take to get to Karsa. It was threatening rain, and so humid that I hoped a monsoon burst would explode, and cool me off in the process. The walk was via the raised Campuhan Ridge, which led to the village of Bangkiang Sidem.

I walked down the laneway at the Ibah resort, and crossed the bridge, where a many-roofed temple rose above me like a magnificent slender tree, its roofs extending one under the other like the skirts of a striated pine tree. Then I started climbing. It was hot, and hotter and then hotter again. I had left it a little late to depart Narasoma, and now found myself hurrying along, at greater speed than I would have liked in that sluggish heat; concerned that my slot might go to someone else if I did not turn up right on time. The rice fields fell away below like waterfalls of green, as I hurried along the spine of the ridge, stopping at intervals for a swig from my water bottle. The sky was low and very grey.

When I arrived at Karsa, I was sweating and panting, and gulping at my remaining water. It appeared that most people who attended there did not arrive on foot. There was a road that met it at the other side, and minibuses and taxis were intermittently unloading unflustered-looking people; trans-fers booked from their hotels and guesthouses. I took a few minutes to recover my breath before going towards the reception area, then stood by the entrance, looking around.

Karsa was a beautiful Balinese complex of thatched roofs, ponds with pink and white water lilies, and palm trees. Behind were the terraced rice fields, knee high now, verdant and lush with all this rain. The stone pathways had mosaics of flowers set into them. There was a scent of incense and a faint chiming of bells.

I made myself known, and then sat in the usual open air reception space of Asia, with rattan couches, drinking the lemongrass tea I was offered. I filled in a form, which wanted to know what sort of oil I would like to be used in my massage, among other things. I looked again at the description of the massage I was about to have.

'Your massage begins with Reiki which opens your aura and chakras to receive divine healing energy throughout your treatment. Reiki also brings your therapist into their highest state so they are totally present and focused on you and your experience.' I had no idea what any of that phraseology meant. This was not my language, nor my world.

Several of us were waiting on the rattan chairs and couches to be called for treatments, and several more staff members making their way among us, yet our collective noise was no more than a murmur. There was universal background silence, apart from the soft chiming of bells, until one of the large nearby ponds started thrashing unexpectedly and violently. Something was exploding out of the water like missiles, then sinking rapidly from sight again, leaving the surface silent and flat and ominous.

It was catfish, I realized after a startled minute or so. When I was finished with the tea and the forms, I walked over to the pond where the huge ugly catfish were stalking their own, moving beneath the murky surface and then lunging into the air every so often, hurtling towards each other with something like malevolence. The pond was deep, and I found myself taking a couple of steps back from it. I felt as I did at a cliff edge: a sensation of vertigo where gravity seemed to be propelling me ever forward, although I was standing still. I could not stop watching the catfish. They were the antithesis of everything Karsa seemed to represent: peace, contemplation, safety.

'Madame?' a young woman softly called to me. It was my masseuse.

I followed her along the mosaic paths, into a thatched hut. There was a showerhead in one corner, and a massage table, which had a neatly folded sarong on it. She left me to undress. I lay face down on the massage table as directed, staring at the stone floor through the hole in the table, waiting for her to return. I could still hear the infrequent pulsing of the catfish in the distant pond.

I had decided that I would ask my masseuse to explain what she was doing as she worked, but I soon discovered she did not speak English, other than a few sparse essential words. The vocabulary was to be all in her confident, fluent hands.

'OK?' she said, before beginning.

'OK,' I said, and closed my eyes.

For a while, I felt nothing, but sensed her hands hovering some inches from my body, as if they were a divining tool waiting to twitch towards some source. Even in that humidity, I could feel the extra layer of heat her hovering hands made above my skin. Then, after about five minutes, she began the massage.

'Too hard?' she asked, pressing down. 'More hard?'

I had never had a proper massage before. I had no idea if she was pressing too hard or not hard enough.

'OK,' I said uncertainly.

For a time, I felt nothing. I knew her hands were there, massaging me, but it felt like white noise: everywhere and nowhere, something far in the background. Then she began to work on my shoulder blades, each one in turn.

I felt that. Pain began to suddenly stab through me, with increasing velocity. It was excruciating. I couldn't speak. I was too taken aback to ask her to stop. I closed my eyes even more tightly, not that I could see what she was doing anyway, and gritted my teeth. I had never physically experienced anything like this in my life. It felt as if she was literally sticking first her fingers into a space near each shoulder blade, and then as if both her hands were actually inside my body, searching for something. It felt like she was digging, excavating, trying to tug at something, I thought, almost comatose with pain. I squawked involuntarily.

'OK?' she said, pausing temporarily.

I was unable to reply. I was definitely not OK, but I could not summon any words. I felt barely conscious.

She kept going; I have no idea how long for. The session lasted ninety minutes, but if you had told me later that it was actually as short as ten minutes or as long as five hours, I would have believed either: time was elastic and strange and febrile in that thatched hut. As she stood over me, I had an image in my head of a surgeon's hands, deep and deft within an opened body, where no human hands usually go. It felt like she had made two holes, one at each shoulder blade. With bewilderment, I realized it felt as if she was looking for something, or trying to pull at something. I also realized I was close to passing out with pain; I was in a fog of utter physical agony.

Then she moved her hands upwards. Suddenly I felt an unexpected light weight; a weight that started at my shoulder blades and extended some distance down my back on either side of my spine. The pain stopped.

I thought her hands were still fluttering on my back, where I felt that odd, unidentifiable weight, until she gently tapped on my forearms with both hands, to explain that she was finished. She indicated she would leave the room, and let me shower and dress, but that I was to rest for a few minutes first. I was confused. Her hands were now right in front of my face, not pressing against my shoulder blades, where I knew for certain there was now some almost insubstantial weight that had not been there before.

But was it weight? I wondered, as she left. I wasn't sure now. I had had the strangest sensation and conviction that something had been physically wrenched, tugged at, then pulled out of my body and laid lengthways down across my back, starting at my shoulder blades. *Wings*, I thought with sudden incredulity. I feel like wings have just been forcibly yanked out of my body, where they had been lying hidden and crushed, then shaken out and folded carefully across my back. I stared at the ground. I didn't believe in any of this. I don't believe in any of this. But what just happened there?

Back in the little reception area, I sat down once again and was brought more lemongrass tea. I watched as other people arrived back from their treatments in various other huts in the Balinese compound. They looked happy and serene and calm. I felt shaky and peculiar and feral.

Along with the tea, I had been given the same feedback form on a clipboard that everyone else around me was now filling in. There were several questions that I had absolutely no idea how to answer.

How was your massage today?

Would you recommend us to other people?

Is there anything we could improve upon at Karsa?

What was I going to write? That at the end of my intuitive heart massage, which had been physically agonizing, I had felt like wings had been pulled out of my body? Really? If I had read this sort of review myself, I would have thought, with merriment, what sort of mad lunatic wrote that? I left the forms blank.

On the way out, I walked past the catfish pond, and the fish rose up as one in a chorus of noise, falling back as a writhing black fountain.

The next day was my last in Bali. My rucksack was packed. I had already extended my visa once. I was leaving for Kuala Lumpur that afternoon, and a few days later, would move on to Los Angeles. But as I tidied up Marigold, I kept wondering if I was ready to leave this place. Or, more accurately, ready to start the slow return journey back to Ireland. The truth is, I never feel ready to go back to Ireland, which is why I always want to keep leaving it. There is a German word, *Sehnsucht*, which means 'a longing and yearning in the heart for travels that have been and travels yet to come'. That's what will always be in my heart. There is so much richness already in my life from my travels, and there will always be the solace of elsewhere.

I put on my swimsuit for my last swim in the Narasoma pool. Standing at the top of the steps that led down to the empty pool, I felt the familiar thrill of anticipation, and hurried down them one last time. In the blue sunlit water, I swam.

I thought again about what the fortune teller in Yangon had told me about love and marriage, and that, whatever happened,

I would be OK. It had not been what I had wanted to hear about my future, but as I swam, I realized that not only was I going to be OK in the future, but that I already was more than OK. I was entirely happy again. Elsewhere had mended me; had performed its unique sorcery, as it always does; had allowed me to find a perspective and a peace I had needed so badly.

Our lives so often don't turn out the way we think they will. Or mine didn't, anyway. Not having children was never what I wanted, but it is what happened. At some point, the tears have to end, otherwise you begin to damage your own life with grief. And although it was never what I wanted, it is what I have now, and I have learned life is too short to waste part of it in eternal regret of an absence, whether of a lost love or an unborn child. I am not a parent, but I still do have many things in my life that I treasure. My freedom and independence. My time. I can go where I like, and do what I wish. I have choices about what to do with my time, and that is a rare privilege in our society. There is a deep value in having such latitude within a life; a life I do not take for granted.

In the Narasoma pool, I found myself thinking again about the arcane experience at Karsa the day before. As I swam those sixteen strokes back and forth, into my head unbidden came an image. It was of the blue wooden box at home in my living room, at the other side of the world. The box I had bought all those years before; where my old passports were kept; the box that was painted with an image of a red-haired woman on a horse, flying through a starry night. Flying with silver-edged wings, I recalled with startled amazement, as I stopped swimming, and began to laugh with sudden delight.

Acknowledgements

Thank you, Julie Reynolds-Martinez, my Nieman Hanger Sister. The amazing non-stop conversations on our crazy, fabulous, hilarious road trip in California, Arizona and Nevada in February 2016 were the catalyst for the idea for this book.

Thank you, Tanya Sweeney; who's always all over the zeitgeist, has brilliant ideas, and is breathtakingly well read. After that road trip, several people helped me figure out what I was trying to write, but the person I owe by far the most gratitude to is you. Over a year, we met regularly in each other's homes for working dinners to critique each other's work. Along with the necessary food, wine and gossip, Tanya spent most of that time trying to show me how I had to suppress the reporter within so I could listen to, and trust, my own voice. I know I got by far the better bargain in our ad hoc writing group of two.

Thank you to my former partners: the three people named here as Lewis, Jake and Dex. Nobody ever embarks on a relationship thinking they are one day going to feature in a memoir. I asked each of you if I could tell the particular, sometimes very difficult, stories recounted in these pages, and I acknowledge with gratitude your individual permissions to do so. But each of you also knows that beyond what's written here there were so many joyous, prodigious and unforgettable stories that we created in our time together. Sempre, indeed.

Thank you, Cáitríona Corcoran, my beloved sister; dear friend; wise counsellor; steadfast supporter; and, rarest of all in anyone, the kindest and most non-judgemental of individuals.

Thank you, Brian McIntyre, my essential friend, who gave me the word *fernweh*, and so much else. Including *rattenfreude*.

Thank you, Róisín Ingle, the most creative, dynamic and charismatic person I know, who came up with what I immediately knew was going to be my title: Elsewhere. We will always be there for each other.

Thank you, Selina Guinness. The greatest gift of my travels has been the extraordinary people I met along the way, and the friendships that continued long after. We've been telling each other stories since we first met in Poland back in 1993, and I'm so happy to know we'll never stop.

Thank you, Beth Williams. Oh my. We've gone through a lot since running into each other in India in 1995. We survived the rickshaw crash in Delhi together, and so much else since then. And we're not done yet.

Thank you, Eileen Lyons, my pirate friend from forever. You heard some of these stories on our latest road trip – through Alice Munro country in Ontario; in Wingham and Bayfield, and Clinton, where we found the Formica time capsule of Bartliff's Bakery.

Thank you, Brian Leyden and Carmel Jennings. The funniest, kindest and best of friends; the most generous of hosts; the part-time keepers of the Beast of Ballyconnell.

Thank you, Ellen MacNally. We fought the fight together for such a long time. Nobody except us will ever know what that was like.

ACKNOWLEDGEMENTS

Thank you, Patrick Freyne, for rescuing my sanity many times over coffees or pints; and for all the great conversations about our respective work: the writing we do both inside and outside of Tara Street.

Thank you, Kathy Sheridan. I have constantly aspired to try and be a fraction of the journalist you are. I am so proud to call you a friend.

Thank you, James, Matt and Alice Ryan. So much stardust left to you three as a legacy; enough for three lifetimes.

Thank you to those additional members of my Nieman family who encouraged, listened, read, gave feedback, and advised as I blundered along with this project. Andrea Simakis and Dorothy 'D' Parvaz; my two other Hanger Sisters: you have enriched my life so much through your friendship; nobody but nobody can make me laugh like you two and Julie. Thank you, Tommy Tomlinson: who would have guessed when we were roaming round Cambridge, Harvard Yard and the Lippmann House that we would one day be swapping drafts of our memoirs with each other. Thank you, Kael Alford, for those chats on the way to Plum Island and Bob's Lobster. Thank you, Susan Arnott, pretty much an honorary Nieman to me, for your necessary wisdom and friendship during my time in Cambridge, and ever since. Thank you, Rose Moss, whose thought-provoking writing class I took for one semester. Thank you also to all my other Nieman brothers and sisters in our class, for making that year extraordinary and unforgettable.

Thank you, Robert 'Bob' Giles, former curator of the Nieman Foundation for Journalism at Harvard University. You selected us 2009 Nieman Fellows and in so doing gave our class both a transformative experience and lifelong friends from across the globe. You sent us back to our newsrooms inspired and determined to keep telling important stories. Veritas for ever. I will always owe you, Bob.

Thank you, Fiona Murphy, editorial director at Transworld Ireland, and my editor on this book. You have been such a careful, thoughtful and inspiring editor to work with. Also at Transworld, thank you to Patricia McVeigh, Aimee Johnston and Hayley Barnes for publicity; designer Beci Kelly for the cover work; and to Orla King for her contribution.

Others who helped and supported throughout in varied important ways: Jennifer Bray, Helen Comerford, Oliver Comerford, Charlie Connelly, Julie Cruickshank, Chris Delaney, Katie Donovan, Brenda Fitzsimons, Joyce Hickey, Ciara Higgins, Declan Jones, Brian Kilmartin, Jude Leavy, Sarah McCann, Belinda McKeon, Madeleine Moore, Mary O'Malley, Yvonne Nolan, Janet Pierce, Hope Reese, Rosie Schapp, Veronica Walsh, Joseph Woods and Oonagh Young. Thank you all so much.

And of course, thank you to my lovely and loving extended family, the Bolands and Corcorans, in Clare, Galway, Kerry, Dublin and elsewhere; with a special shout out to my niece Lara Morawiec in Bristol, and to Giles Lord.

About the Author

Rosita Boland is a senior features writer at the *Irish Times*, specializing in human interest stories. She was a 2009 Nieman Fellow at the Nieman Foundation for Journalism at Harvard University. She won 'Journalist of the Year' at the 2018 Newsbrands Ireland journalism awards.